Dundee

THE CITY GUIDE

THE
LIST
GUIDES
SCOTLAND

DUNDEE
ONE CITY, MANY DISCOVERIES

DUNDEE
ONE CITY, MANY DISCOVERIES

Edited by Catharina Day & Sarah Milne
Catharina Day is a writer, interior designer and the author of three guide books including *The Cadogan Guide to Ireland*. She has lived with her family near Dundee for over 20 years

Contributors: Stephanie Cantrell, Helen Chalmers, Fiona Danskin, Mark Fisher, Tom Sampson, Kirstyn Smith
Design: Gavin Munro
Advertising Sales: Aimi Gold

Images courtesy of: Alan Dimmick, Cara Pirie, Dundee City Council, Forestry Commission Scotland, University of Dundee, University of Dundee Museum Services, VisitScotland Angus & Dundee, VisitScotland/Scottish Viewpoint and individual venues listed

© 2010 The List Ltd
ISBN: 978-0-9557513-2-5

Published by The List Ltd
Head Office:
14 High Street
Edinburgh EH1 1TE
Tel: 0131 550 3050

Printed and bound by Scotprint, Haddington

Contents

Welcome to Dundee

As an honorary Dundonian, and someone who is very proud to live in Dundee, it's a huge pleasure to be introducing this unique guide to you.

I first came to Dundee back in the mid-80s with my (now) husband. On our first date he invited me to a Dundee United match. I fell in love with him, with the city and of course with my beloved football team.

I have seen enormous changes in Dundee over the past twenty-five years. It has always been a wonderful place to live, but there has been a real renaissance in the city and there's a feeling of optimism for the future.

Dundee is the perfect base to explore some of the most beautiful parts of Scotland.

I never tire of that stunning view over the Tay, and the city has so much to offer.

We have gems like the newly refurbished art gallery and museum at The McManus and the wonderful Discovery Point.

I celebrated my 50th birthday with my closest friends and family on board the RRS Discovery. It was a night to remember with fantastic food, wonderful wine and a unique atmosphere.

Then there's the DCA, Sensation, Verdant Works and the country's only Observatory open to the public. Not to mention two thriving universities and the world renowned and ground breaking work going on at Ninewells hospital.

You can shop 'til you drop, and there are more and more good restaurants and pubs springing up all the time, as well as a buzzing nightlife.

With so much to see and do, it's impossible to include everything in just one guide. I hope you make your own discoveries about Dundee when you visit the city for yourself. I did and it became my home.

Lorraine
lorrainekelly.tv

How to use

Within each category, entries are arranged alphabetically and contain the following information:

Address & telephone number
■ All entries are located within Dundee, unless otherwise indicated

Opening hours
■ Opening hours are correct at time of going to press. For a restaurant or café, a distinction is made between opening hours and food served hours, if applicable

Description
■ A general description of the establishment, attraction or activity, with relevant information on its style, atmosphere, clientele, facilities and services offered

Westport Gallery
■ 48 Westport, 01382 221751; Mon–Sat 9am–5pm. Closed Sun

A sophisticated Aladdin's cave, Westport Gallery sells an array of arty pieces. Known and named for its artwork, a variety of prints and pictures are available at the gallery including amazing digital shots and paintings of the bridges over the Tay and other Dundee landmarks.
wpgal.co.uk

Website for the area, venue or business
■ Where possible a website is provided (minus the www.), where more information should be available

THE BYZANTIUM

MEDITERRANEAN CUISINE

Sophisticated Casual Dining in Dundee.

For reservations please call

01382 221946

t. 01382 221946   a. 13 Hawkhill, Dundee, DD1 5DL
w. byzantiumrestaurant.com

Attractions 12-23

Culture 24-39

Activities 40-51

Shop 52-63

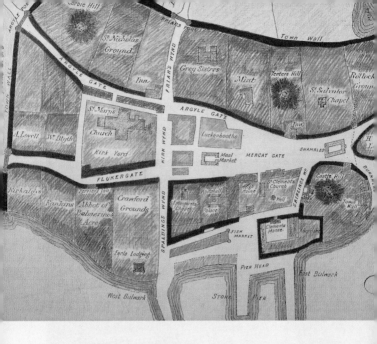

A brief history of Dundee

The site we now know as Dundee was first used in the Mesolithic era by a population that no doubt appreciated the sunny climate and natural harbour. By 1100, a clear settlement had emerged. The name of the city has its origins either in the Celtic Dun Dhia, 'the hill of God', or the Latin Dei Donum, 'the gift of God'. William I of Scotland granted Dundee to his brother David, Earl of Huntingdon, in around 1200, and the town was dedicated to the Virgin Mary, symbolised today by lilies on the coat of arms. David built a church to honour her. He also encouraged trade in wool and hide with the rest of Europe.

Wars with England followed periodically as succession and territory were fought over.

IN CELTIC DUN DHIA MEANS 'THE HILL OF GOD'

William Wallace, hero of the war of Scottish independence, was reputed to have been educated here toward the end of the 13th century. Wars and plague struck again and again but the town managed to thrive and trading became more significant, especially the import of timber and hemp from the Baltic and Scandinavia. Many Dundonians were deeply involved with the reformed Christian doctrines. During the time of the English civil war, Dundee was first sacked by the Royalists then, in 1651, devastated by the Parliamentarians under George Monck, when one sixth of the population was killed.

In the 18th and 19th centuries prosperity grew, especially for those in the linen industry, shipping, whaling and, of course,

the manufacture of jute. Dundee benefited from trade generated by the British Empire and bought in raw jute from India. The manufacture of jute products, such as sacking and tents for the British army, created many jobs and the population rose massively. Dundee became a place of over-crowded tenements and smoking factory chimneys. A population of over 90,000 was recorded in 1861.

Dundee also developed a jam industry in the early 20th century as the surrounding areas established soft fruit as a major agricultural product. With the rise of DC Thomson, journalism also grew. More recently the three Js of jam, jute and journalism have gradually been replaced by a new economy, which includes biomedical and biotechnology research and development, and a thriving computer games industry. ∎

Timeline

- **c1200** The town granted by charter to David, Earl of Huntingdon
- **1292** Dundee becomes a Royal Burgh
- **1620** The city is now Scotland's second largest importer of wine
- **1651** Dundee devastated by English forces under General Monck
- **1797** Beginning of the Keiller marmalade industry
- **1815-1840** The harbour commission is established, with planned improvements to the harbour including the creation of docks for deep water ships.
- **1820** The first bales of jute arrive from India
- **1824** Dundee police force established
- **1833** Verdant Works established
- **1879** The Tay Bridge disaster
- **1901** RRS *Discovery* built by the Dundee Shipbuilding Company
- **1920** The closure of the Dundee Shipbuilding Company
- **1966** The Tay Road Bridge opens
- **1967** Queen's College becomes independent from St Andrews as the University of Dundee
- **1974** Ninewells Hospital opens
- **1985** RRS *Discovery* returns to the city and becomes the focal point of the reinvention of Dundee
- **1994** University of Abertay founded
- **1996** Cyclacel, a biotechnology company, is founded, one of a cluster in Dundee
- **1998** The last jute mill closes
- **1999** Dundee Contemporary Arts opens
- **2000** Sensation opens
- **2010** The McManus reopens after four years of renovation

Attractions

Whether you're looking for an exciting family day out or want to learn more about the history of the city, Dundee has plenty of attractions to suit everyone. Celebrate Dundee's maritime heritage, the arrival of jute and the new scientific excellence found in this inspiring city.

DUNDEE
ONE CITY, MANY DISCOVERIES

Located in Dundee's cultural quarter, **DCA** is home to: a world-class **EXHIBITION SPACE** where entry is always **FREE**; the city centre's only **CINEMA** – showing new releases, classic movies, independent filmmakers, opera, world cinema and films chosen by you!; a state-of-the-art **PRINT STUDIO** with a great range of workshops; cutting-edge design, jewellery and gifts in our **SHOP**; limited edition prints and publications in our **PRINT SPACE**; great food in our **RESTAURANT** and a lively buzz in our **CAFÉ BAR**. Get involved at www.dca.org.uk or find us on Twitter and Facebook. Pick up your RED card today & start saving points to spend at DCA cinema!

Broughty Castle Museum
■ Castle Approach, Broughty Ferry, 01382 436916. Mon-Sat 10am-4pm; Sun 12.30-4pm. Oct-Mar: closed Mon
dundeecity.gov.uk/broughtycastle

See Culture, page 34

Claypotts Castle
■ Broughty Ferry, outside access available at all times

Claypotts Castle is a terrific example of a 16th-century Scottish z-plan towerhouse. With square rooms astride its towers as well as the original roof, Claypotts was once owned by John Graham of Claverhouse, 'Bonnie Dundee', who was killed at the Battle of Killiecrankie in 1689. Located in the middle of a housing estate off the main A92 Arbroath Road, just east of Dundee.
historic-scotland.gov.uk

↘ **Bonnie banks** Claypotts Castle was once owned by the Jacobite 'Bonnie Dundee'

Andrew Lothian
Andy is chief executive of Insights, a global learning and development organisation that he co-founded with his father in Dundee over 20 years ago.

'Dundee offers great heritage attractions. Dundee Heritage Trust offers two world-class visitor attractions – Captain Robert Scott's iconic ship, RRS *Discovery* and Verdant Works. These are internationally renowned assets and we need to take more advantage of them.'

Gregg Wighton
Age 20

'Dundee is a city just waiting to explode!'

RRS Discovery

■ Discovery Point, Discovery Quay, 01382 309060. Apr-Oct: Mon-Sat 10am-6pm; Sun 11am-6pm; Nov-Mar: 10am-5pm; Sun 11am-5pm. Closed Dec 25/26 & Jan 1/2; Admission: £7.50 (discounted joint ticket with Verdant Works available)

RRS *Discovery* was built in Dundee for Captain Robert Scott's scientific exploration of Antarctica and it is one of the city's greatest attractions. Catching your eye as you arrive by car or train, it has become the perfect focus for the regeneration of Dundee. A leisurely visit exploring the boat and the excellent museum is a sure way to be transported back to that great venture, its scientific discoveries, adversities and successes.

The 47-man crew are the stuff of legend and you can glean a mass of fascinating detail about their trip not only from the vessel itself, but also through displays of scientific discoveries and artefacts from the voyage. Several films bring to life the first

"AN EXHIBITION OF IMAGES OF THE VAST ICEBOUND STRETCHES THAT MANAGED TO TRAP THE DISCOVERY, MAKE FOR COMPELLING VIEWING"

expedition, started in 1901, explaining the aims, expectations and characters involved. Images of the vast icebound stretches that managed to trap the *Discovery* make for compelling viewing. The ship is in wonderful condition, giving a tremendous insight into how the crew lived and how the scientists worked once they were aboard. Everyone got the same food but not the same accommodation and, whatever their rank, they had to endure the cold and boredom of being stranded for months in the ice.

The *Discovery* was built with the expertise of Dundee's shipyards, well used to building strong whaling ships. It went on to make several more trips to Antarctica, adding to the scientific data collected on the first voyage.

The attached café often doubles as a small gallery space, with changing exhibitions throughout the year, and the foyer offers a wealth of tourist information for Dundee and the surrounding area.
rrsdiscovery.com

◥ Discover and do
RRS Discovery was built for Captain Scott's famous scientific expedition to Antarctica. The ship remains in wonderful condition

The Law

Stuart Purvey and Stevie Anderson, along with brothers Simon and Martin Donald, formed rock band The Law in 2004 and have gone on to achieve success and acclaim for their music. All are proud Dundonians. thelawmusic.com

'Dundee has some pretty cool tourist attractions. The *Unicorn* is one of the oldest ships in the world. It gets overshadowed by *Discovery* – but as Britain's oldest floating frigate it's still really cool. The Mills Observatory is another gem and you don't just have to go to see the stars – we have great memories of hanging around Balgay Hill in our younger days with our heads in the clouds.'

Dundee Central Library
■ The Wellgate, 01382 431500. Mon/Tue & Thu/Fri 9am–6pm, Wed 10am–6pm, Sat 9.30am–5pm

Dundee Central Library is an oasis for family records and local history (including a collection of William McGonagall works, see page 20). Check out the free monthly concerts in the Wighton room featuring works from the library's own collection of early Scottish music. This is the place to find out what is going on in the city: many venues in Dundee host classical ensemble concerts on a sporadic basis. Dundee Central Library is the busiest public library in Scotland and Dundee City Council's most visited public building.
dundeecity.gov.uk/library/central

◥ **Heads down** Dundee Central Library is an excellent resource for residents and visitors

Mills Observatory
■ Glamis Road, Balgay Park, 01382 435967.
dundeecity.gov.uk/mills

See Activities, page 47

◳ Ships in the night HM Frigate Unicorn was built in 1824

HM Frigate Unicorn

■ Victoria Dock, 01382 200900. Apr-Oct: Mon-Sun 10am-5pm; Nov–Mar: Wed–Fri noon-4pm; Sat–Sun 10am-4pm. Closed Mon/Tue. Last admission 30 minutes before closing. Admission £4; concession (under 15s, students, senior citizens) £3; children under 5 free; family (2 adults, 2 children) £11; family (1 adult, 2 children) £9; group (10 or more) £2.50 per head

Billed as the world's oldest floating wooden warship, this wooden frigate is an anomaly in a world of shiny buildings, its ornate unicorn figurehead rearing up majestic and proud. Built in 1824, the ship was saved from a watery burial by a few enthusiasts, now the Unicorn Preservation Society. It is incredible to walk the decks of a warship built for sailing and to see the tough and cramped conditions within. The 18-pounder guns and the paraphernalia of the sailors littered among the modern notices add to the authenticity, as does the cold if you visit in winter. She survived because the Napoleonic wars finished and she was no longer needed for battle. Instead the hull was built over and training became her purpose. **frigateunicorn.org**

Sensation Dundee

■ Greenmarket, 01382 228800.
Mon–Sun 10am–5pm. Last
admission 4pm. Admission
£7.25; special needs adult
£5.75; child (4–15) £5.25;
special needs child £4.25;
OAP/student £5.25; under 4s
free

Explore the science of the five
senses through interactive shows
and exhibits in this bright ten-
year-old space. It is close to the
railway station, shopping and the
DCA and there's ample parking
nearby – all pointing to a great
place for a family day out.
Sensation appeals to both children and adults, its exhibitions
covering a wide spectrum of
science presented in an exciting
fashion. Interactivity is the order
of the day, with plenty of red
buttons for little hands to press
and games to get involved in.
Serious science is covered in an
engaging way and there are
temporary exhibitions and talks
throughout the year.

The modern Infusion Coffee
Shop sells light meals and
hosts free discussions led by
scientists from Dundee
University every second
Wednesday of the month at
6pm. This is just one of the
ways the university reaches out
to Dundonians.
sensation.org.uk

William McGonagall

Considered by many as the
worst poet ever, and hailed by
others as a comic genius, the
self-educated McGonagall
spent most of his life as a
weaver in Dundee. He took up
verse in his 50s, never made
much money and died penni-
less. Despite being the butt of
many jokes and insults, he was
the eternal optimist and his
memoirs report no moments of
self-doubt. He aspired to be the
next poet laureate after
Tennyson and famously
walked from Dundee to
Balmoral to ask the queen. He
was turned away. His verse is
banal and so bad it is funny. He
tackled romantic subjects –
disasters, heroic deeds, as well
as Dundee events such as the
collapse of the Tay Rail Bridge
(see opposite) when he wrote:
'The cry rang out all around the
town/Good heavens! The Tay

Bridge has blown down.'

His simple declamatory
work is still read. In 2008,
some of his poems sold at
auction for £6,700, not bad for
a despised wordsmith. Lines
from his poems are inscribed at
various sites in Dundee (see
above) and a collection of his
work is housed in the Central
Library.
dundeecity.gov.uk/mcgonagall

⬎ A bridge too far The Tay Road and Rail Bridges span the river

The Tay Bridges

Many people who have never even visited Dundee will still have heard of the Tay Rail Bridge disaster. The bridge linked Dundee and Fife, but collapsed in gale-force winds as a train was crossing it on 28 December, 1879. Everyone on board was lost in the cold waters of the Tay. The new bridge, opened in 1887, is still in use today and was designed to withstand future gales. Fourteen workers died during its construction. William McGonagall (see panel opposite) in a poem to the second Tay Bridge wrote, in his inimitable way:

THE TAY RAIL BRIDGE OPENED IN 1887, IS STILL IN USE TODAY

'And your thirteen central girders which seem to my eye/Strong enough all windy storms to defy.'

That bridge gives wonderful views. The road bridge is less splendid but very practical, bringing the motorist straight into Dundee city centre. Road-planning teams in the 1950s and 1960s created this traffic flow and in the process were accused of turning the city centre into a concrete wilderness. The current plan is to lessen the impact of the road bridge by shortening the concrete ramps in the proposed waterfront redevelopment.

Verdant Works

■ West Henderson's Wynd, 01382 309060. Apr–Oct: Mon–Sat 10am–6pm; Sun 11am–6pm; Nov–Mar: Wed–Sat 10.30am-4.30pm; Sun 11am-4.30pm. Closed Mon/Tue. Closed Dec 25/26 & Jan 1/2. Last admission one hour before closing. Admission £7; concession £5.25; child £4, family (2 adults, 2 children) £19. Discounted joint ticket available with Discovery Point

Set in the heartland of Dundee's jute factories, this fascinating attraction describes the jute industry and the impact it had on the city, where the hard life of the mills has left a permanent stamp. Before jute's prominence in 19th-century Dundee, the weaving industry had long brought in new blood, especially from Ulster. With the addition of jute, imported from India, Dundee grew massively. Women and children made up the bulk of the employees because they could be paid less. The displays and films within Verdant Works illuminate the history of 19th- and 20th-century Dundee, its links with India and the lengthy process of making jute. There is also a permanent exhibition on the much-loved Broons. **verdantworks.com**

WOMEN AND CHILDREN MADE UP THE BULK OF THE EMPLOYEES

⬊ **Hey jute** Verdant Works gives an insight into the jute industry

Churches of Dundee

The churches of Dundee contain some architectural gems and only a small selection are mentioned here. The oldest building in Dundee (c1480) is St Mary's Tower, also known as the Old Steeple Tower, which contains a wonderful peal of bells. The buildings are now divided between two churches. It is worth checking out the beautiful stained glass windows in St Mary's, which include designs by Burne-Jones and William Morris. St Paul's Cathedral in the High Street was built by architect Sir George Gilbert Scott in 1855 on the site of an ancient castle.

The high altar mosaic is by Salviati of Venice and some panels in a carved wood cabinet date from the 16th century. The medieval-style St Salvador's was designed and furnished by George Bodley, Scott's brother-in-law. It is a superb example of gothic decoration, richly painted with stencilled patterns in red, green, blue and biscuit. The classical St Andrew's on King St (1774) was funded by the influential Dundee trade corporations, whose history is detailed on the website. St Andrew's Cathedral (1836) is also worth a visit.

■ **St Andrew's Cathedral**, Nethergate, 01382 225228. standrewscathedral.co.uk

■ **St Andrew's Parish Church**, King Street, 01382

◥ **Tower of song** St Mary's Tower is the oldest building in Dundee, dating from 1480

224860. standrewschurch. btinternet.co.uk

■ **St Mary's Parish Church**, Nethergate, 01382 226271. dundeestmarys.co.uk

■ **St Mary's Tower**, Nethergate. See website for opening times. dundeestmarys.co.uk

■ **St Paul's Cathedral**, 1 High Street, 01382 224486. stpaulscathedraldundee.org

■ **St Salvador's**, Church Street, Hilltown, 01382 221785. Call for opening times

Culture

Dundee is a city that's rich in culture, both historical and contemporary. From the beautifully refurbished McManus to the theatrical traditions of the Rep, this is a city that punches way above its weight in the arts. Exhibitions, contemporary dance and public art all help enrich the cultural landscape.

DUNDEE
ONE CITY, MANY DISCOVERIES

Art

Bonar Hall
■ Park Place, 01382 345466

A gift from a generous benefactor to the people and University of Dundee, Bonar Hall is used as a venue for occasional public lectures, films and amateur performances, but is mainly the setting for conferences and private parties.
bonarhall.co.uk

Duncan of Jordanstone College of Art & Design
■ 13 Perth Rd, 01382 385330. Open during college hours

The college has a formidable reputation as one of the UK's best art schools and there is a constant stream of cutting edge exhibitions on offer at various locations throughout the campus

⬂ Art at Duncan of Jordanstone

and beyond – the Cooper Gallery, the Lower Foyer, the Bradshaw Gallery, the Matthew Gallery and Centrespace at the DCA. Each has a different emphasis and shows work by students, teachers and international guests.
Themes for the exhibitions often link in with other disciplines taught in the university and the aim is is to get students aware of how best to show their work.
An ideal time to visit is the graduate show at the end of the summer semester.
exhibitions.dundee.ac.uk

Public Art

Dundee City Council has had a policy of commissioning visual art since 1982 and the results are placed all over Dundee for everyone in the city to enjoy. The locals are fond of this art and it is fun to see the delighted expressions of children in the city centre when they discover the coiling bronze dragon and the comic giant Desperate Dan with Minnie the Minx and Gnasher in the pedestrianised area. Their irreverent style is so different from the mighty 19th century statue of Queen Victoria plumped on a pedestal outside the McManus. Travelling around the city, you will find a variety of sculptures in metal and stone, as well as mosaics – currently there are 120 pieces of public art scattered around Dundee. Among the most elegant are the pair of deer leaping the hedge in the Technology Park. There is also an Anthony Gormley sculpture in the garden of Maggie's Centre at Ninewells Hospital.

⬎ **For an art lover** The striking DCA is a cultural hub for the city

Dundee Contemporary Arts (DCA)

■ 152 Nethergate, 01382 909900. Gallery opening times: Tue-Sat 10.30am-5pm; Thu 10.30am-8.30pm; Sun noon-5.30pm. Closed Mon

Since opening in 1999, the DCA has become a favourite venue and meeting place for all generations. The centre combines an excellent gallery and workshop space, a popular café bar (Jute) and a cinema showing world and arthouse films. Inside, there's a sense of space and sophistication. The conversion of this old warehouse by Richard Murphy Architects has created a light and attractive building in which many different activities can happen at the same time. As well as the two cinemas, there is a print-making studio open to all (often offering low-cost courses), as well as resources for making digital videos. At street level, the angular frontage blends well with the surrounding architecture because of the use of muted colours mixed with copper, glass and wood. Inside, the high ceilings, white walls and large windows make it an enjoyable venue to spend time in. The gallery shows work from major international contemporary visual artists in a series of exhibitions throughout the year. Many visitors head straight downstairs to Jute and the cinemas, making it a bustling venue, particularly on Friday and Saturday nights. **dca.org.uk**

Life Sciences

Sir Philip Cohen is a leading researcher and academic who has lived in Dundee for nearly four decades. His work has attracted some of the best scientists to the city, and he has fundraised more than £80m over the last ten years for research into life sciences.

'Dundee is widely recognised as one of Europe's strongest centres for life sciences and biotechnology and – with thousands of scientists working in these areas – this sector accounts for 16% of the local economy. Today, there are 4,300 people working directly in life sciences and biotechnology in Dundee and thousands of other jobs in the service sector are dependent on it. Dundee is no longer the city of jute, jam and journalism, but the city of biochemistry,

biomedicine and biotechnology. The annual research income of the college of life sciences in 2009 reached nearly £50m – a far cry from the mid-1970s when I nearly had to close down my laboratory for the lack of £1,000. In addition to the usual ingredients of success (hard work, perseverance, capitalising on opportunities and occasional good fortune), it was the enormous amount of effort put into recruitment that was crucial for the success of the college of life sciences at Dundee. A place is only as good as the people who work in it and the appointment of team leaders, who were not only outstanding scientists but also prepared to put in the huge effort needed to develop the enterprise and build up world-class infrastructure and equipment, was critical to the city's success in the industry.'

Eduardo Alessandro Studios

■ 30 Gray Street, Broughty Ferry, 01382 737011. Mon-Sat 9.30am-5pm. Closed Sun

This gallery sells contemporary Scottish art, rare and sporting prints and also has as a workshop framing pictures. Well-known local artists sell their work here and it is always worth going along to see the selection of Scottish landscapes.
eastudios.com

Generator Projects

■ 25-26 Mid Wynd Industrial Estate, 01382 225982. Thu-Sun noon-5pm. Admission free

This space provides an opportunity for unknown artists and art students to show their work. Funded by the Scottish Arts Council and the City Council, it is run by artists and open to everybody. The flexible space is used for making and showing visual art, exhibitions, films and performance.
generatorprojects.co.uk

Hannah Maclure Centre

■ University of Abertay Dundee, Top Floor, Abertay Student Centre, 1–3 Bell St, 01382 308324. Mon-Fri 9.30am-4.45pm. Admission free

This is an exciting space showing around five exhibitions a year, in addition to displaying projects of staff and students, and hosting other events. It explores the use of new technologies to make artworks and embraces interdisciplinary collaborations. As well as the gallery, where international artists are shown, there is a cinema showing world films, open to the public on Friday afternoons, a cinema club every other Tuesday and a coffee bar. **hannahmaclure centre.abertay.ac.uk**

❧ **Up on the roof** Top-floor terrace at the Hannah Maclure Centre

↘ **Cultural heart**
The McManus has reopened after a four-year closure for refurbishment both inside and out. The results are breathtaking

The McManus: Dundee's Art Gallery & Museum

■ Albert Square, Meadowside, 01382 307200. Mon–Sat 10am–5pm; Sun 12.30–4.30pm. Admission free

The people of Dundee are delighted to have this wonderful venue back after its four-year closure for refurbishment. Reopened in 2010, the new formal gardens and pedestrianised street around the entrance have made a huge improvement to the exterior. The galleries inside are impressive in a grand Victorian way – the building was designed by Sir Gilbert Scott as a memorial to Prince Albert. In the 19th century, Dundee's jute barons did their civic duty by donating British and European art for the collections and succeeding curators have continued to add modern works, especially those by Scottish artists. The colourists and the Glasgow

"THERE IS SOMETHING FOR EVERYONE HERE FROM GREAT PAINTINGS TO THE SKELETON OF A HUMP-BACKED WHALE"

Lorraine Kelly

Lorraine is a Scottish television presenter and journalist best known for her morning show on GMTV. She lives in Broughty Ferry and is an avid Dundee United supporter.

'I am one of the patrons for the refurbishment of the McManus Galleries and it is going to be the jewel in Dundee's crown. All the upheaval has been worth it after the biggest facelift in its 138-year history. Locals and visitors alike will enjoy seeing Dundee's story told in an educational, inspirational and entertaining way.'

Boys are well represented and there are some stunning Victorian paintings. The modern gallery spaces have been integrated well with the traditional. Each gallery has a theme; Landscapes and Lives, for example, includes local archaeology and natural history artefacts as well as a vivid depiction of the changing flora and fauna over hundreds of years of shifting climate and the settlement of man. Here you'll see a long boat hollowed out from a huge tree. There is something for everyone in here – great paintings, booty from the empire, local history displays, a rare Jacobite flag and the skeleton of the great humpbacked whale which in 1883 dared to swim up the Tay. It was chased northwards by expert Dundee whalers, harpooned to death and later sold at auction for £226. The new café sells coffee and light meals with the added bonus of fine stained glass windows to look at.
mcmanus.co.uk

The Queen's Gallery

■ Queen's Hotel Buildings, 160 Nethergate, 01382 220600. Mon-Fri 10am-5.30pm; Sat 10am-5pm. Closed Sun

Close to the DCA, this small gallery shows paintings, applied arts and sculpture. There is a new show every month and the owners have a good eye for selecting the work of both established and emerging artists.
queensgallery.co.uk

Roseangle Gallery

■ 17 Roseangle

The ground floor of this house is home to Dundee Art Society, champion of traditional visual art in the city. The members show their work in spring and autumn and the gallery is used at other times for private shows. DAS opens up its gallery to all artists for an exhibition before Christmas and again in the summer to coincide with the art school's graduate exhibitions. The society also runs a variety of

↘ Dundee's WASPS Studios

art workshops, and talks throughout the year.
dundeeartsociety.co.uk

WASPS Studios

■ Meadow Mill, West Henderson's Wynd

Part of this old mill contains the studios of working artists. Once a year the artists throw open their studios and invite the public to visit and see their work in progress and have the chance to buy some – see website for latest open studios dates.
waspsstudios.org.uk

↘ **Coming up roses** Dundee Art Society exhibit at Roseangle Gallery

* Proposed new site for V&A

↘ **Riverside tales** The V&A will be at the heart of the new waterfront regeneration

V&A at Dundee

This very exciting development is planned for 2014, when London's V&A Museum will open the V&A at Dundee. The site will be built jutting out into the Tay, and is part of a massive regeneration scheme to reconnect the city with the river and its beautiful watery landscape. The centre aims to be a source of inspiration and research for design in Scotland and hopes to foster the growth of its creative industries. The exhibitions are likely to attract huge numbers and have a positive effect on business and tourism in Dundee. The city should become a destination for those who want to see world-class exhibitions on design styles and concepts. The project has already brought the V&A, Dundee City Council, the University of Dundee and Abertay University into a close working partnership, boding well for a beneficial collaboration between the creative arts, academia and industry in the city. The creative arts and design are already very strong at the universities and in the digital entertainment industries in the city. Despite the current downtown in the economy, the £47m project is still on track and promises to be of immense prestige, boosting the attractiveness of Dundee in many ways.
vam.ac.uk

Sir Mark Jones
Director of the V&A

'V&A at Dundee will be a rich resource for the design and creative industries, attract visitors to world-class exhibitions, and be a significant contributor to the economic development of Dundee. The V&A at Dundee will have continuous appeal to visitors, researchers and students of design. Dundee has an international reputation for design. We hope the V&A at Dundee will be an exciting part of the city's regeneration, help define and develop what is best in Scottish contemporary design and offer inspiration for the future.'

Culture

⬇ The scenic Broughty Castle

Broughty Castle Museum

■ Castle Approach, Broughty Ferry, 01382 436916. Apr-Sep: Mon-Sat 10am-4pm; Sun 12.30-4pm Oct-Mar: Tue-Sat 10am-4pm; Sun 12.30-4pm. Closed Mon. Admission free

This fortified medieval building is central to this picturesque village overlooking the Tay. Inside, winding stone steps lead to exhibitions on the local area, military history, the colonial era and wildlife. It is fun to climb to the lookout room and take in the excellent views over the Tay, these days spotting dolphins, not warships. The gem here is The Orchar Collection of Scottish Victorian art, which includes paintings by William McTaggart, whose work was immensely successful in his lifetime, and other artists of the Scott Lauder school, depicting mainly genre and rural scenes. There is also a charming painting of a girl by the 20th-century society portraitist, Philip de Laszlo, and a farm-yard scene by James McIntosh Patrick. The shop sells post-cards and outside there are defences and fortifications to investigate. **dundeecity. gov.uk/broughtycastle**

D'Arcy Thompson Zoology Museum

■ Carnelley Building, University of Dundee, 01382 384310. Open on Friday afternoons during the summer holidays, otherwise by special request. Occasional evening lectures, check website for details

Sir D'Arcy Wentworth Thompson is best known for his 1919 book *On Growth and Form*, an elegantly written work, which is still an inspiration to biologists today. He was the first professor of zoology at Dundee and spent most of his academic life here, collecting a fascinating array of specimens and leaving them to the university. His interests were diverse and ran to maths, biology and the classics. **dundee.ac.uk/museum/zoology**

⬇ The Zoology Museum

⬎ **Doctor in the house** The Tayside Medical History Museum

Tayside Medical History Museum
■ Ninewells Hospital Foyer, Ninewells Hospital, 01382 384310. Admission free

Exhibits in this intriguing museum include cupping glasses, X-ray goggles and mustard oil. Run jointly by the university and NHS Tayside, it documents the tradition of medical excellence in the region. It is possible to walk from here along to Maggie's Centre, designed by Frank Gehry (see Architecture, page 39). Because Maggie's is a centre for cancer patients it is not open to the general public, however the exterior is easy to see without getting in the way and its inspirational design is a tonic for us all. **dundee.ac.uk/museum/medical.htm**

University Museum Collections
■ University of Dundee, 01382 384310. Admission free

If you are in the city for a longer stay, it is worth visiting these collections, housed in various venues across the campus: there's a mix of fascinating scientific artefacts, zoological and botanical specimens and art from the 17th century onwards, including some Celtic revival and the Scottish colourists. As the university does not yet have a permanent museum building, the work is displayed during university hours in the Tower Foyer and Lamb Galleries in the Tower Building, with more displays in the Carnelley Building, Bonar Hall, the Chaplaincy Centre and the Dental School. Contact Museum Services for further information, as opening times are limited.
dundee.ac.uk/museum

Verdant Works
■ West Henderson's Wynd, 01382 309060
verdantworks.com

See Attractions, page 22

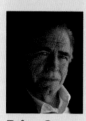

Brian Cox

Brian is an Emmy award-winning stage and film actor who's appeared in films such as *The Bourne Supremacy*, *The Ring, Troy* and *X-Men 2*. He was born in Dundee in 1947.

'The Dundee Rep was really pioneering. It was where I started my theatrical career and developed my interest in acting when I was a teenager. The Rep itself really marked the card for the whole idea of what a rep was. The old building actually burned down but the wreck is still there. In fact, I've been back and found the spot where I used to put up posters.'

Theatre

Caird Hall
■ City Square, 01382 434940 (box office)
cairdhall.co.uk

See Nightlife, page 78.

Dundee Rep
■ Tay Square, 01382 223530

The theatre that brought us the Proclaimers musical *Sunshine on Leith* is unique in the UK for supporting a permanent ensemble of actors. In 1999, then-director Hamish Glen secured a National Lottery grant to support fourteen actors for three years. The scheme was a success and continues to this day under the artistic directorship of James Brining and associate director Jemima Levick. What it means for audiences is more actors on stage and, because of longer rehearsal times, a better standard of production. There is also a pleasure to be had in seeing familiar faces tackling unfamiliar plays. What it means for the actors is the opportunity to hone their skills and develop ties with the resident Scottish Dance Theatre, the community company and the city at large. The 70-year-old company, which gave Brian Cox his first break, offers a broad repertoire of its own in addition to the visiting programme of stand-up comedy, dance and drama. Hits have ranged from the elevated drama of Howard Barker's *Scenes from an Execution* and Ibsen's *Peer Gynt* – both big winners in the Critics' Awards for Theatre in Scotland – to the singalong backstage musical *Gypsy* and the reliably high quality Christmas show.
dundeereptheatre.co.uk

↘ **It's a Rep** The Dundee Rep is world-class

The Space

■ Kingsway Campus, Dundee College, Old Glamis Road, 01382 834934

The Space is an RIBA award-winning multi-purpose venue. Those making the first claim are the students enrolled in the Scottish School of Contemporary Dance, which offers three- and four-year full-time degree courses and has close ties with Scottish Dance Theatre, the country's leading professional company, based at Dundee Rep. Since the opening of the Space in 2002, the students have been making use of three bright, airy and interlinked dance studios – with their double-height ballet barres – as well as the flexible theatre itself. Flexibility is the 200-seat theatre's strength. As well as performances from the likes of Scottish Ballet and Stephen Petronio, it is used for shows by students on the theatre arts course, who often collaborate with the dance students. The two-floor building with its distinctive curves is also a great facility for Dundee as a whole.
dundeecollege.ac.uk/SSCD/Venue

↘ **Breathing Space** Interior of The Space

Gary Robertson
Gary is an author and street poet from the city. He writes in the Dundee dialect and has achieved far-reaching acclaim for his work.

'The arts have come a long way in Dundee. It's brilliant to see more and more young people keen to get into performing and having the facilities to do so at modern venues like the Space or the Scottish Dance Theatre. I think we'll see more of this in the future, which will really put Dundee on the map.'

Culture

Whitehall Theatre

■ 112 Bellfield Street,
08717 029 486

An independent, commercially run theatre in a 1920s art deco building (look out for the murals) which relies on the goodwill of volunteers to supplement the work of the small core staff. Split between 500-seat stalls and 250-seat balcony, the theatre presents a busy bill of popular entertainers, musical favourites, stage comedies, stand-up comedians, larger-scale children's shows and musicals from local amateur dramatics societies as well as the occasional modern dance company. The bright 72-seat café looks onto the trees in the small grassy square adjacent to the theatre entrance.
whitehalldundee.co.uk

Architecture

Dundee may not previously have been known as a place of architectural interest, but today's cityscape is much more inspirational, and plans to develop the waterfront will carry this forward. Dundee today is mostly a mix of Victorian (the recently refurbished McManus) and 20th-century buildings (the Frank Gehry-designed Maggie's Centre, pictured). From the medieval period until the 18th century Dundee grew rapidly as a trading port. Dudhope Castle, Claypotts and Broughty Castle and St Mary's Tower survive from these times and the restored Gardyne's Land on the High Street includes a 16th-century merchant's house. Many 19th-century textile mills survive – a quick walk round Blackness demonstrates their modern uses, or a trip to Verdant Works (page 22) shows off a mill's original purpose. There was a lot of demolition in the city in the mid-20th century, especially the mill workers' tenements. The impressive

Caird and Marryat Halls and Council Chambers were built around a piazza in the 1930s. The car-dominated waterfront is now being redeveloped. New buildings will create an environment far more in sympathy with the river than those built in the 1960s and 1970s. The universities are contributing to vibrant new building in the city, and it's worth seeing the magnificent restoration of the 19th-century façade of Morgan Academy, which was almost destroyed by fire in 2001. Close by, Baxter's Park, designed by Joseph Paxton, contains a fine sandstone pavilion.

Activities

From gentle city walks and lively skate parks to golf and football, Dundee has a range of activities for all levels of energy. The compact nature of the city means that whatever activity you want to try out, it's all within easy reach. Just get your trainers on and go.

DUNDEE
ONE CITY, MANY DISCOVERIES

Ancrum Outdoor Education Centre & Clatto Water Sports Centre

■ 10 Ancrum Road, 01382 435911. Opening times and prices vary according to activity

This organisation offers courses in a variety of sports and activities, including blokarting (also known as land karting), climbing, gorgewalking, rafting, sailing, mountain biking and winter sports. The centre runs courses throughout the year as well as offering adventure weeks for children. The instructors are fully qualified and you can hire good quality equipment. The courses often take place in locations such as the Tay and the glens. The centre has a video and navigation room where it holds preparatory sessions. **ancrum.com**

TRY BLOKARTING, GORGEWALKING, SAILING AND CLIMBING

⬎ Clatto Water Sports Centre

Avertical World Climbing Centre

■ The Old Church, 7-11 Blinshall Street, 01382 201901. Mon-Fri noon-10pm; Sat/Sun 10am-7pm. Admission variable. Equipment can be hired on site

Situated in an old church, this climbing centre offers abseiling as well as challenging, intermediate and easy routes for all levels of climbing. It provides a broad range of courses for all abilities, holds many competitive events in the winter and allows you to book private and group sessions. Children from age four and above are welcome (along with a proficient adult), and there is a well-stocked shop with helpful and expert assistants. **averticalworld.co.uk**

Balgay Park

■ Balgay Hill

A rich assortment of trees and shrubs and fine views of the Tay make this park a very attractive haven right in the middle of Dundee. There is lots of wildlife here – listen for woodpeckers along the twisting paths which make it feel like a wild space, rather than a municipal park. The recently restored Hird Bridge links the park with Balgay cemetery. Spanning a natural gorge, it was built in 1879, just after the park opened as a recreation ground for mill workers. The park includes Victoria Park, a rose garden and a pitch and putt course as well as the Mills Observatory (page 47).

Broughty Ferry Beach

A lovely place for a stroll or serious walk, and only a short bus ride from Dundee city centre. The Blue Flag beach starts close to Broughty Castle and you can walk for miles northwards along the sand, enjoying the great views across the estuary, towards Tentsmuir Point and back towards Dundee. The award-winning Barnhill Rock garden is a nice diversion en route, with some comfortable benches for picnicking. After an afternoon of fresh air and exercise, you could explore the snug little pubs, cafes and craft shops among the attractive old streets and alley-ways of this old fishing town.

Camperdown Country Park

■ Coupar Angus Road, 01382 431818; Camperdown Golf Course, 01382 431820; Camperdown House, 01382 431850; Countryside Ranger Service 01382 431848. Admission free

This lovely old estate on the edge of Dundee is a favourite place for walkers and their dogs, covering about 400 acres and housing 190 species of tree. It

↘ Camperdown Country Park

incorporates Templeton Woods and Clatto Reservoir, linked by paths for those who would like to walk or cycle. Camperdown House is impressive, but it is not open to the public. It was built in 1828 and forms an elegant centrepiece to the park. Keen gardeners will certainly be inter-ested in the mutant Camperdown Elm, from which thousands of grafts have been made. So far it has escaped Dutch elm disease. **camperdownpark.com**

Parks and open space

In a city with such an industrial background, it may be surprising to hear that over a quarter of Dundee's urban area is open space of one sort or another, from country parks to local green spaces. Dundee City Council and other agen-cies recognise that public open spaces contribute a tangible benefit to residents' quality of life, and as such Dundee's green places are well-kept and have a sustainable future within the cityscape. The local community also see this as a priority, and Dundee Trees & Woods in Greenspace (TWIGS) works with everyone within the community to help improve the green environment in and around Dundee City Centre. For a full list of Dundee's parks, see the website. **dundeecity.gov.uk/ leisurecomms/parksgardens/**

■ **Dundee Trees & Woods in Greenspace** dundeetwig.com
■ **Dundee Public Open Space Strategy** dundeecity.gov.uk/leisurecom ms/pos

Camperdown Wildlife Centre

■ Coupar Angus Road, 01382 431811. Mar–Sep: Mon–Sun 10am–4.30pm; Oct–Feb: Mon–Sun 10am–3.30pm. Admission £3.50 (adult)

An award-winning wildlife centre can also be found at Camperdown. It is a great day out for the family, and the centre has 50 different species of animals, including wolves, brown bears and lemurs. A new visitor centre and café is due to open in summer 2010. **dundeecity.gov.uk/ camperdown/**

Clatto Country Park

■ Dalmahoy Drive, 01382 435911 (for water-based activities) and 01382 436505 for any other query

This was built as a reservoir and now provides a great opportunity for water sports. Back on dry land, beside the water you'll find easy walks, a children's play area and picnicking and barbeque sites. The Ancrum Outdoor Education Centre (see page 42) runs water-based courses here.

Cycling

Dundee is well-equipped with plenty of cycle paths (page 100), and it is easy to hire bikes when visiting (page 107), making pedal power a great way to get around.

DISC (Dundee International Sports Complex)

■ Mains Loan, 01382 438804. Mon–Fri 10am–10pm; Sat 10am–6pm; Sun 10am–9pm. Fitness studio opens Mon–Sat from 8am. Admission prices vary

This centre hosts national competitions and runs a variety of fitness classes, and besides the fitness suite it has facilities for five-a-side football, table tennis, bowling, volleyball, netball, and badminton. **dundeecity.gov.uk/ sportscentres/disc.htm**

Dundee Botanic Garden

■ Riverside Drive, 01382 381190. Mar–Oct: Mon–Sun 10am–4.30pm; Nov–Feb: Mon–Sun 10am–3.30pm; coffee shop: Mon–Sun 9am–5pm. Admission £3; children £2; senior citizens £2; family (2 adults & 2 children)

↘ **Dear green place** Dundee's Botanic Garden is a haven in the city

£8. Entry for university staff and students is free

Swap the hustle and bustle of the city for a slice of tranquillity at Dundee Botanic Garden. The gardens are a spectacular green space with areas for different plant habitats. From the tropical rainforest glasshouse, with banana trees, citrus fruits and a pond with giant water lilies, to Sir Garnet Wilson's sycamore, which was the only tree on site when the garden was started and is named after the lord provost of 1940–46, Dundee Botanic Garden provides year-round enjoyment. Particularly worth a look is the garden of evolution, with its impressive dry stone walls and its explanation of the evolution of plants. In the native plant area you can see the variety of plants grown in Scotland. The coffee shop is popular for home-made cakes and soups and the adjacent plant sales area is perfect for a nosey around. The garden sometimes hosts open-air performances, so call ahead for upcoming events.
dundee.ac.uk/botanic/

Dundee Law
■ Law Road

Dundee Law is an extinct volcano, standing proud above the city. The Law is the city's most distinctive landmark, and for many years was central to Dundee's defences. Once home to an Iron Age fort, it now has a memorial for the two world wars standing at the summit. The Law is most notable for the breath-taking panoramic views it offers. On a clear day, visibility stretches over 45 miles of scenery across the city itself,

➘ **Bird's-eye** The Law has excellent views across the city

Fife, the Tay Estuary, Perthshire and the Sidlaw hills. The summit is reachable by car, bike or foot – the steep climb is not for the faint-hearted. Fact panels frame the observation point, offering visitors historical and environ-mental information and the view at night is mesmerising. The Law is a must-see for visitors and locals to truly appreciate Dundee's unique location.

The Factory Skatepark
■ 15 Balunie Drive, 01382 509586. Mon-Fri 10am-10pm; Sat 9am-8pm; Sun 10am-8pm. Admission £6 for two hours; £3 for beginner sessions

Besides having fabulous indoor skateboard, roller blade and BMXing facilities, the Factory Skatepark offers basketball, an internet café and an Indian restaurant. For the young and active this is a great venue for all levels of ability. The Factory was purpose-built to give youngsters a well-maintained space to practise in, rather than having to improvise in abandoned buildings. You can enjoy fully supervised beginner sessions, book coaching sessions and hire equipment. There are girls-only sessions to encourage girls to participate. During term-time, the skateboarding runs alongside complementary and often free activities allowing primary school children to combine a supervised homework session with 45 minutes of furious physical activity. Workshops are run on such diverse subjects as graffiti art, healthy lifestyle and photography. Elsewhere in the city Dudhope Park Skatepark is outside, free and open during daylight hours.

factoryskatepark.com

Golf

There are some excellent golf courses in Dundee (page 99), meaning you don't have to travel far to enjoy a perfect round.

Ice Arena

■ Camperdown Leisure Park, 01382 889369

Perfect for a rainy day, the Ice Arena is well established and award winning. It offers lessons for all ages and public sessions where equipment can be hired. It also hosts the occasional evening show in a swirl of sequins and disco lights. All of the staff are trained to a very high standard and are happy to

Games Industry

Dave Jones is creative director and founder of Realtime Worlds, and has been responsible for the creation of some of the world's best-selling video games, from *Lemmings* to *Grand Theft Auto*. Realtime Worlds is based in Dundee.

'For anyone who hasn't visited the city recently, Dundee might seem an unlikely location to be one of the world's hubs of cutting-edge gaming technology, but it really has gone through a massive transformation in the last decade.

'Its vibrant student population comes from having two excellent universities in the city and of course includes the world-renowned games,

computer arts and related degrees at Abertay University, which in turn feed into the city's fifteen games development studios. All combine to make a big contribution to a city that has reinvented itself with restaurants, nightclubs, arts centres and galleries. Yet most things in Dundee are still convenient enough to get around without a car, contributing to a city with very little in the way of traffic or air pollution problems. And when our staff do want to escape the city, they don't need to be up at 6am, they can head for the hills in less than an hour and spend the day snowboarding, hillwalking or mountain biking.

'But keep watching this space – Dundee's transformation is far from over.'

help with any queries. The Ice Arena provides a brilliant day out for all ages.
dundeeicearena.co.uk

Lochee Swim Centre
■ St Mary's Lane, Lochee, 01382 431840. Open every day, times vary according to school term times and holidays. Admission £2.60 (swim only)

This medium-sized swimming pool also has a fitness suite and sauna. **swimlochee.co.uk**

Mills Observatory
■ Glamis Road, Balgay Park, 01382 435967. Apr–Sep: Tue–Fri 11am–5pm; Sat/Sun 12.30–4pm; Oct–Mar: Mon–Fri 4–10pm; Sat/Sun 12.30–4pm

Reach for the stars at the UK's only full-time public observatory. The sandstone building was a gift to the people of Dundee, donated in 1935 by linen manufacturer and keen amateur scientist John Mills. Entry to the observatory is usually free, other than the planetarium shows, which project a simulated night sky onto the domed ceiling, showing thousands of stars and the Milky Way. Two display areas show models and pictures of the solar system in addition to local information and historical equipment – including the original telescope used at the observatory in 1935. The main viewing telescope is upstairs, and there are also a variety of smaller telescopes and binoculars for visitors to

❯ The Mills Observatory is a great family day out

use on the viewing balcony. By day, the balcony offers fantastic views of the river and surrounding areas. Mills Observatory appeals to astronomy lovers and novices alike. Part of the Dark Sky Scotland programme.
dundeecity.gov.uk/mills

Olympia Leisure Centre
■ Earl Grey Place, 01382 432300. Open every day, times vary. Call or check the website for most up to date information. Admission prices vary

Olympia Leisure Centre consists of a large fun pool which is very popular with children and families because of its waves, rapids and chutes. There is a baby pool and a training pool for quieter swimming and there's also a fitness suite. At the time of writing, the centre is due to close in 2013, and be rebuilt in a different location in order to free up the site for the proposed waterfront redevelopment.
swimolympia.co.uk

SEE THE ORIGINAL TELESCOPE USED IN 1935

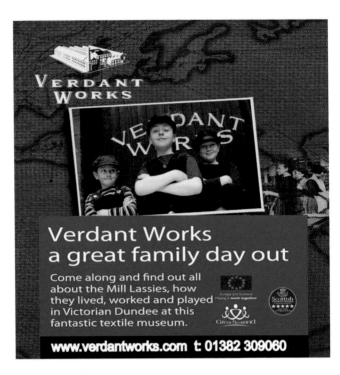
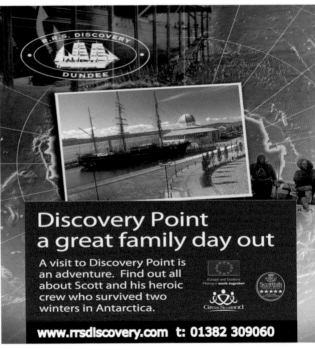

Football

To some people Dundee is famous for being the city with the two professional clubs with the closest grounds in the UK. When it is said that it is possible to kick a ball out of Dens Park and land it in Tannadice it is barely a lie. So why two clubs? Both Dundee and Dundee United have a proud, long and independent history. Although it is fair to say United have been in the ascendancy in recent times it was not always thus. Dundee's heyday was the 1960s, winning the league in 1962 and getting to the semi-final of the European Cup the next year, a pattern that was repeated by United in the 1980s. Dundee has suffered in recent years from a torrid spell of financial misery but there are signs of better times. Hopefully both clubs will be playing in the Premier League and the derby will again become one of the highlights of the city's sporting calendar.

■ **Dundee Football Club**, Dens Park Stadium, Sandeman Street, 01382 826104, dundeefc.co.uk

■ **Dundee United Football Club**, Tannadice Park, Tannadice Street, 01382 833166, dundeeunitedfc.co.uk

Peter Hadden
Peter is a keen football fan and lived in the city for 20 years

'The football scene in Dundee is quite unique. I think it's because there's no geographic (both stadiums are in the same street), religious or class divide between who supports which team. It might be more to do with age: the older folk remember the Dundee glory days of the sixties and the younger people tend to remember the United glory days of the eighties. The point is that the fans of both sides socialise together before and after games – I don't think that happens in many other cities.'

Gemma Watson
Age 24

'You can't beat a day out at Camperdown Park, especially when it's sunny'

Activities

McManus Collections Unit
Guided Tours 2010

From birds to butterflies, coins to costumes and fossils to foreign artefacts, the Collections Unit offers visitors a fascinating glimpse into Dundee's museum collections.

Tours are free and available on selected dates. Booking essential. Tel 01382 307200. Booking line open **Mon to Sat 10am - 4.30pm** or email: **themcmanus@dundeecity.gov.uk**

McManus Collections Unit
Barrack Street
Dundee DD1 1PG

www.dundeecity.gov.uk/events

Dundee CHANGING FOR THE FUTURE

Soccerworld

■ Old Glamis Road, Dundee;
01382 816888

Whether it's a kickaround with mates or a five-a-side league, Soccerworld caters to all. With eight new pitches of artificial turf, players of all ages and abilities can start perfecting their skills. To make the experience even more Premiership, teams can enter into a league, with prizes to be won each season. A sports bar for parents, showing all major games, keeps everyone happy.
soccerworlduk.com

Swannie Ponds

■ Stobsmuir Park,
Pitkerro Road

Popular with locals who come to see the ducks and swans that live happily here and provide plenty of entertainment, the two ponds are surrounded by pathways and beautiful grass banks, daffodils and lots of spring blossom trees. When they get tired of spectators, the birds have a well-planted island to hide in. It is possible to go boating on the ponds.

Tay River Trips & Dolphin watching

■ 01382 542516, Apr–Oct.
For times and prices see website

These sightseeing and wildlife tours in the Tay Estuary are run by voluntary organisation Taymara, which trains volunteers how to handle a boat safely. The bottlenose dolphins have come to the area in recent years, and no one knows whether they will stay here permanently. The boats

◥ Lucky visitors will spot dolphins

do not chase the dolphins, but their seemingly inquisitive nature means the dolphins often approach the boats of their own accord, bow riding and putting on acrobatic displays. If you don't want to get on a boat, one of the best vantage points for dophin watching is Broughty Castle ramparts.
tayrivertrips.org

Walking in Dundee

Walking is a wonderful way to absorb the character of this city. Dundee has a beautiful river-scape, with views across to Fife, and stretches of it have been developed for walking close to the water. Other places to walk are Balgay Hill and Victoria Park, where there are tall trees, bird-song and flowers, or the Law, a volcanic hill topped with a war memorial. Camper-down Park is gener-ously set with paths and stately trees. You can forget you are in a city there and walk for hours. A visit to Dundee Botanic Garden is a delight, the paths meander around well-planned and well-kept sections, and you can retreat into the glasshouses if the weather turns bad. A short walk around the city centre takes you to the Howff, the ancient burial ground given to the city by Mary Queen of Scots. The grave-stones give a great insight into the occupations of the people over centuries.

THE HOWFF WAS GIVEN TO THE CITY BY MARY QUEEN OF SCOTS

Activities

Shop

With a proud tradition of independent traders, Dundee has an inspiring mix of shops of all sizes, making for a vibrant city centre. Coffee merchants, hunting supplies, a kitsch tartan tea cosy and designer brands – you can find them all within a few steps of the Overgate and Wellgate shopping centres. A spot of retail therapy is definitely in order.

DUNDEE
ONE CITY, MANY DISCOVERIES

❯ Fresh from The Apple Tree

The Apple Tree
■ 129 Nethergate, 01382 223020. Mon–Sat 9am–5pm. Closed Sun

The Apple Tree is known locally for being a classic yet affordable accessories shop. Although its main clientele are middle-aged professionals, there is something to suit all generations. Particularly worth having a look at is the range of chunky costume jewellery, while statement scarves and handbags are also excellent. If you want to shop in style, head to the Apple Tree. **vivaldiaccessories.com**

Arkive
■ 36–40 Seagate, 01382 206615. Mon–Sat 9.30am–6pm; Sun noon–5pm

Formerly Ozzy's, now Arkive, this large, bright shop is a self-confessed 'lifestyle store'. With high fashion and street style, Arkive caters for everyone from preppy to skater. An open-plan shop floor is staffed by assistants happy to help you negotiate your way from Diesel to Carhartt; G Star to DCs. The Boardroom sells skate gear and accessories, with some exclusive brands, as well as a spray paint section for street artists and art students. There is a sizeable female section providing funky hoodies, dresses and a rainbow of skinny jeans. Accessories such as Skull Candy headphones and surfer-style necklaces are scattered around the shop's nooks and crannies. With such a wide range of fashions, it is difficult to find fault with this on-trend store. **ozzys.co.uk**

Big Bairn Books
■ 17 Exchange Street, 01382 220225. Tue–Sat 10.45am–4.45pm. Closed Sun & Mon

An Aladdin's cave of Dundee's literary history. Specialising in annuals and comics from DC Thomson, the publishers of *The Beano, The Dandy, Oor Wullie* and *The Broons*, it is a quiet celebration of the place that added journalism to Dundee's three Js. The shop also offers classic Scottish literature and a selection of second-hand books. Come in to while away time in this hidden gem.

❯ On-trend street style at Arkive

Shop

Dundee Dialect

There are many strands of the Dundee accent, the most extreme being unfathomable. However, many Dundonians adopt a softer version which may still take time to get accustomed to.

In formal terms the Dundee accent most noticeably substitutes the monophthong /e/ in place of the diphthong /ai/. Thus, 'eye' becomes 'eh', 'my'– 'meh','pie'– 'peh', 'fiver'–'fehver' and so on. The best known Dundonian phrase to demonstrate this is 'eh'll hae twa plehn pehs an' an ingin' ane an' a', translating as 'I'll have two plain pies and an onion one as well' (Dundee is also well known for pies …) You will be forgiven for thinking there is an unfeasibly large number of men in Dundee called Ken. Don't be misled. Ken is 'to know', such as 'eh, ah ken' (yes, I know), or punctuates the end of a sentence to ascertain whether the listener has understood. Good sources for more on the Dundee accent are listening to Dundonian singer Saint Andrew (saintandrew.biz) on songs such as 'It's Good To Be Alehv, Is It?', and the now out-of-print 'Dundonian for Beginners' by Mick McCluskey. You should be able to find a copy in the local library. Or as they would say in Dundee, the 'lehbray'.

Shop

The Cheesery

■ 9 Exchange Street, 01382 202160. Tue-Fri 9.30am-5.30pm; Sat 9.30am-5pm. Closed Sun

Since opening in January 2008, Dorothy Hegarty's delightful wee cheese shop (the first of its kind in the city) has been quick to make its mark, winning Dundee Retail Awards' Newcomer of the Year, and quickly gathering many regular customers. There are over 50 cheeses, 20 from the British Isles, the most local being the Anster from St Andrews. The southern beauties hail from the likes of Snowdonia and Cornwall, while among the continental cheeses you will find the unashamedly smelly Epoisse from Burgundy. The Cheesery is

◥ The delightful Cheesery

also a great showcase for other local produce – handmade oatcakes from Cupar and Carnoustie, ceramics from St Andrews and many preserves and chutneys. If you're looking for a wedding cake with a difference, Dorothy can supply you with a magnificent tiered 'cheese' cake, made up of whole wheels of differing sizes of cheese. Bright and welcoming. **thecheesery.co.uk**

⬦ **Arts and crafts** The DCA shop stocks high-quality design objects

DCA Shop

■ 152 Nethergate, 01382 909900. Mon-Sat 10.30am-5.30pm; Thur 10.30am-8.30pm; Sun noon-4.30pm

This exciting design shop is possibly the best of its kind in Scotland. With one side being entirely glazed, this light and airy space creates the perfect showcase for the finest contemporary design. The high-quality, innovative work on sale includes jewellery, textiles and ceramics both decorative and practical. It's encouraging to see such a strong focus on home-grown creative production together with other UK and international designers and makers. You will also find highly desirable household goods from larger design companies such as Marimekko, and Joseph Joseph, select stationery goods, greeting cards and art magazines. For children, there's a great range of unusual toys and craft projects, while kids' books by local illustrators can be found among the thoughtfully stocked staircase bookshelf. The staff are helpful and knowledgeable about the represented designers and artists, and can advise those on a tighter budget about their 'Own Art' scheme, which makes investing in a beloved piece of art or design more affordable. **dca.org.uk/shop/index.html**

Fisher and Donaldson

■ 12 Whitehall Street, 01382 223488. Branches also at 300 Perth Road, and 83 High Street, Lochee. Mon-Sat 8am-5.15pm. Closed Sun

Everyone loves a bun, and some of the finest to be found in these parts are at this fourth-generation family bakery. Alongside the essential Dundee cake and its award-winning British apple pie, Fisher and Donaldson also bakes sumptuous wedding cakes. Whether a coffee tower or a steak

bridie whets your appetite, the cheery staff are on hand to help. If you have trouble choosing, its in-house café is the perfect place to sample some tasty treats.
fisheranddonaldson.com

Gows

■ 12 Union Street, 01382 225427. Mon-Sat 9am-(just before) 5pm. Closed Sun

Gows certainly caters for a niche market but is well established in Dundee, trading since 1860 and stocking almost everything the field sport enthusiast could ever need, from guns to binoculars, rods to waterproofs. The staff at Gows are very knowledgeable about their subject and will advise customers unsure of what to purchase. If you are especially interested in fly fishing, it's worth going to see their vast range of related products.
gows-secureshop.co.uk

Grant's Butchers

■ 187 Blackness Road, 01382 669 556. Mon-Sat 7.30am-5.30pm. Closed Sun

The walls of awards bear testimony to the quality and popularity of Grant's Butchers. An important part of the community since 1875, with a knowledgeable staff of just ten people to cater to their ever-growing range of clients, Grant's provides many local businesses as well as a steady flow of regulars. With beef, pork and lamb sourced from Scotch Premier Meat, Inverurie, it projects a sense of pride in the produce. This is reflected in its

Scottish Federation of Meat Trades awards, from the sublime – its pork, cheese and chive burgers, to the ridiculous – the curry-inspired lamb bhuna bangers. Another local favourite is the Balmoral Chicken – neat parcels of chicken fillets stuffed full of haggis. As well as freshly sourced meat, a number of other products can be enjoyed, from the convenience food – pots of soup, stew and steak stir-fry, to apple and rhubarb tarts made fresh daily.

↘ Unique gifts at Indigo House

Indigo House

■ 69 Perth Road, 01382 206726. Mon/Tue & Thu/Fri 10.30am-5.30pm; Sat 10.30am-5pm. Closed Wed & Sun

Full of curios from owner Ian Smith's travels, Indigo House is a treasure trove. Each find is innovative, recycled and natural, from hand-engraved turquoise and moonstone to Tagua jewellery made from nuts. Scarves, sequinned cushions and ornaments are scattered through the shop, which smells wonderful thanks to the scented candles and incense. The perfect boutique for something a bit special.
indigohouseonline.co.uk

THE WALLS OF AWARDS SHOW THE QUALITY OF GRANTS

Groucho's

■ 132 Nethergate, 01382 228496. Mon-Sat 9am-5.30pm; Sun noon-4.30pm

To many a Dundonian, Groucho's is like a much-loved friend. It's moved around a bit since opening in 1976, but seems to have settled down at the foot of the Nethergate. Run by Alastair 'Breeks' Brodie, Groucho's still calls itself a 'disc and tape exchange'. It's the perfect place to adopt your very own Nick Cave or Nat King Cole – most tastes are catered for. Dedicated to public service, Groucho's once had a Bay City Rollers amnesty, where customers could bring in their offending vinyl and smash it in a special box. It was very popular. As you breathe in the comforting aroma of faded record sleeves, you can immerse yourself in a sea of musical genres, browsing through endless CD racks, boxes of vinyl, DVDs and 7" singles – anything from Patti Smith to Patsy Cline. Groucho's is also a concert ticket agency for gigs around the country and runs buses to some larger events.

For local gigs and club nights, info is posted on the notice board, or in flyer racks. Breeks and his knowledgeable staff will always try their best to help with even the strangest requests – check out the 'Don't Ask' section on the shop's website with choice words from people 'two tracks short of a single'. This undeniable city treasure has deservedly won the Dundee Independent Retailer of the Year for the last two years. Happy browsing. **grouchos.co.uk**

TO MANY GROUCHO'S IS LIKE A MUCH-LOVED FRIEND

❧ **Sounds of the city** Groucho's is a mecca for Dundee's music scene

JA Braithwaite Ltd
■ 6 Castle Street, 01382 322693. Mon–Fri 9am–5.30pm; Sat 9am–5pm. Closed Sun

Braithwaite's has been trading since the 19th century, and walking through the door feels like stepping back in time. The tiny tea and coffee merchants is filled with wonderful smells, while the wood panelling on the walls is decorated with coffee sacking and black-and-white photographs of the shop's long history. The staff are quick to welcome customers like old friends and their cheery manner is infectious. For coffee novices, information about the different blends is on hand. Braithwaite's roasts its own beans on the premises using a secret age-old method. In addition to the many varieties of coffee bean, which are weighed out on old, traditional brass scales, Braithwaite's also sells old-fashioned tea tins, mugs and coffee grinders. The wooden floor creaks and the lighting is dim, giving the shop a worn, much-loved feel. Well worth a visit.

Manifesto
■ 78 Commercial Street, 01382 201527. Mon-Sat 10am-5pm. Closed Sun

Manifesto provides one of Dundee's few truly designer clothes shops, offering on-trend clothing from the newest lines available. Its clothes are aimed mainly at the fashion-conscious young professional, both male and female, and the price tags mean students are definitely not the main customer base. It boasts a diverse range of casual

↘ JA Braithewaite on Castle St

clothes by labels including Paul Smith, Armani, Adidas and Replay Jeans. Pay a visit if the usual high street shops are failing to inspire you.

McManus Shop
■ Albert Square, 01382 307200. Mon-Sat 10am-5pm, Sun; 12.30-5pm

The McManus is newly refurbished and quite frankly an unmissable part of any visit to Dundee. To fully appreciate the shop, you really should browse after a tour round the galleries (page 30). It features books on local history, but the impact of the wartime memorabilia and replica items will be lost if you have not visited the exhibitions. **mcmanus.co.uk**

Shop

Missy La La's

■ 6 Crichton Street, 01382 220923. Mon-Sat 10am-5.30pm

Stocking clothing and accessories for the young and fashion-conscious woman, Missy La La's offers pieces with a definite designer twist, but still at high street prices. As exclusive Dundee stockists for a number of lines, it is a refreshing change from the usual suspects. If you fancy sourcing something quirky for your next party, night out or even something different to wear to work, head down here for something you won't find elsewhere.
missylalasboutique.co.uk

The Overgate

■ 01382 314200. Mon–Wed & Fri/Sat 9am–6pm, Thu 9am–7.30pm, Sun noon–5pm

Dundee's newest shopping centre boasts a vast range of shops and eateries. The single-sided mall (the only one in Europe) is flanked by an impressive two-storey curved glass wall, which floods the centre with natural light. Reopened in

⬎ High fashion at Missy La La's

its present form in 2000, the Overgate has brought high-end retailers to the city. Shops represented include department store Debenhams, which sprawls over three floors, as well as high street favourites French Connection, Primark, Office, Gap, Mango, Lush and a bling-tastic Swarovski boutique. Cafés such as Starbucks and Millie's Cookies provide a welcome break from shopping.
overgate.co.uk

Scottish Antiques and Arts Centre

■ Abernyte, Perthshire, 01828 686401. Mon-Sun 10am-5pm

The Scottish Antiques and Arts Centre is a good destination for an afternoon out of the city. Surrounded by beautiful countryside, the substantial centre stocks an eclectic mix of antiques and locally made gifts, including some one-off jewellery pieces and glasswork as well as soaps and toiletries. The café serves lovely lunches and refreshments and all staff are happy to help with any queries.
scottish-antiques.com

⬎ The single-sided Overgate

Stephen Henderson the Jeweller

■ 1 Union Street, 01382 221339. Mon–Sat 10am–5pm

A huge range of big-name jewellery and watches is available from Stephen Henderson. Its tagline is 'whatever it takes' and it prides itself on its team of knowledgeable, dedicated and friendly staff. It also serves hot drinks in the winter, or a cold beer or champagne in the summer to help lubricate your decisions. If you are serious about buying some top-end jewellery in Dundee, this is definitely the place to visit. **stephenhenderson.co.uk**

Sutherlands

■ 90 Nethergate, 01382 224709. Mon–Sat 9am–5.30pm; Sun (Nov & Dec only) noon–4pm

Whereas our capital city is strewn with Scottish shops, Dundee has just the one, but it's a belter. Around for 90 years, and occupying the same spot on Nethergate for over 50 of them, Sutherlands aims to please all. Half of the shop is devoted to the more kitsch side of Scotland, with haggis money banks and Rabbie Burns napkins. The more traditional side offers full highland outfits and kilt accessories, and drinking vessels such as the hip flask or quaich. For the ladies, a fine range of tartan skirts and shawls, and for the bairns, how about a Scotty dog bib? Sutherlands also has a good range of jewellery, all with a Scottish theme, the thistle being a popular motif. There are other places in town to buy a kilt, but no other where you can choose between a Glengarry and a 'See You Jimmy' bunnet. Here's to the next 90 years.

◥ **Day Tripper** For a unique gift, head to the Scottish Antiques and Arts Centre

Taste Fresh

■ 11 Union Street, 01382 224300. Mon-Fri 8.30am-5pm; Sat 9.30am-4pm

Winner of the 2007 Newcomer of the Year at Dundee's Retail Awards, Taste Fresh has since gone from strength to strength. A delicatessen which also specialises in outside catering, it boasts the occasional tasting session and a range of gluten-free products. Choose between olives at the deli and a lovely selection of sandwich fillers. Customer service at Taste Fresh is always impeccable and the owner sources ingredients with great care. **tastefresh.co.uk**

This Little Piggy

■ 185 Brook Street, Broughty Ferry, 01382 770481. Mon-Fri 9am-5pm; Sat 9.30am-5.30pm

With the shop front decked out in a bright Liquorice Allsorts theme, This Little Piggy is child-friendly from the get-go. Indoors, shelves of funky footwear flank a large communal sofa. Spring/summer stock includes cool Geox trainers at the forefront for boys and a line of cute Lelli Kelli sandals for girls. As well as the newest in kids' shoes, jackets and fleeces for the outdoors, it stocks fluffy puppets for younger children. **little-piggy.co.uk**

Dundee Farmers' Market

■ High Street, 01382 434548. 3rd Saturday of each month 9am–4pm

Situated in the heart of the city, Dundee Farmers' Market is a fantastic opportunity to revel in the abundant harvests of Dundee and Tayside. Its location in the midst of the city's main shopping area and close to ample parking proves that a visit to such a market does not have to involve a long trek out to the sticks. Organised by Dundee City Council, the market is an excellent choice for a family excursion, with vendors showcasing the very best of locally sourced produce. It's hard to deny that food just tastes better when purchased direct from the producer at a market stall and the quality on offer at Dundee Farmers' Market doesn't disappoint. The choice is endless, with locally produced cheeses, baked goods, venison, beef, sausages, jams and fruit wines accompanying the usual fresh fruit and veg. Stalls trading fresh fish, home-made soaps, fudge, tartan tableware and, of course, jute complete this wholesome country experience. **dundeecity.gov.uk/ citydevelopment/ economicdev/farmersmarket/**

Wellgate Shopping Centre
■ The Wellgate, 01382 225454. Mon–Sat 9am–5.30pm, Sun 11am–5pm

Dundee's 'other shopping centre', the Wellgate, lacks the shiny newness of Overgate but is not to be dismissed. It hosts a range of decent shops including Bhs, New Look, Claire's Accessories and Argos. The food court upstairs is hardly gourmet dining but is great for a quick bite to eat. Dundee Central Library (page 18) is situated at the back of the building, where the centre also backs onto Hilltown – one of Dundee's oldest areas, currently in the process of regeneration.
wellgatedundee.co.uk

⬂ **Aladdin's Cave** The Westport Gallery

Westport Gallery
■ 48 Westport, 01382 221751. Mon–Sat 9am–5pm. Closed Sun

A sophisticated Aladdin's cave, Westport Gallery sells an array of arty pieces. Known and named for its artwork, a variety of prints and pictures are available at the gallery, including amazing digital shots and paintings of the bridges over the Tay and other Dundee landmarks. The rest of the shop is stuffed with vases, ornate decorations, lamps, lighting and unique pieces of furniture. Clothes shop Diva is connected to the shop, selling dresses and shirts. With prices spanning all budgets, it's definitely worth a visit. **wpgal.co.uk**

Kirsten Dunnett
Owner of Missy La La's fashion boutique

'There's a real buzz about the place. There are so many students and there's a whole youth culture here around the music, nightlife, fashion and art. It's great to have all these young people in the city – the energy they bring is really important.'

William McNeilly
Age 23

'The people of Dundee really make the city and are good fun to be around.'

Calum Morrison
Age 20

'Ye cannae beat the Dundee banter.'

Shop

Eat & Drink

After all that sightseeing, what better way to re-charge than going out for a friendly drink and enjoying a great meal? Dundee has a variety of exciting places to eat, from traditional bakers to contemporary cuisine. With plenty of options you might find yourself spoilt for choice.

DUNDEE
ONE CITY, MANY DISCOVERIES

Agacan

■ 113 Perth Road, 01382
644227. Tue-Sun 5-9pm.
Closed Mon

The decorated tile façade of this
Turkish kebab house is as
distinctive as its reputation for
tender lamb. The rich decoration
– hand-painted tables, paintings
by the owner and displays of
other artists give it a special
atmosphere. It is very small and
you must book to get a table. The
portions are generous and the
salads fresh. There is a takeaway
service too.

Bon Appetit

■ 22-26 Exchange Street,
01382 809000. Mon-Sat
noon-2.30pm, 6-9.30pm.
Closed Sun

Tucked away from the city
centre on quiet Exchange Street,
Bon Appetit could easily be
missed altogether. This would be
a real shame as the homely little
French bistro is one of Dundee's
gastro gems. Husband and wife
team Audrey and John pride
themselves on being passionate
about people, food and wine,
demonstrated in their warm and
amicable service as well as the
attention given to the menu.
Traditional French cuisine is
given a modern twist – a
generous helping of *moules
frites*, fresh from Dundee's own
G&A Spinks, comes with ever-
changing sauces, from a thick
and garlicky mariniere, to Indian
and Mediterranean versions
concocted by John. To follow: a
crisp savoury crêpe, stuffed to
the brim with a selection of
mouth-watering fillings and even
a cheeky glass of pink
champagne, or a false Kir

Eat & Drink

Royale for drivers. Dedicated to
supporting local businesses and
using local produce, Bon Appetit
provides a quiet, quirky
environment to linger over a
truly French dining experience.
bonappetit-dundee.com

Bridgeview Station

■ Riverside Drive, 01382
660066. Mon/Tue & Wed-Fri
8am-4pm; Sat 8am-4pm,
5.30-11pm; Sun 8am-6.30pm

Bridgeview Station, housed in a
Victorian railway station, is
quirky and stylish with a
spacious interior and panoramic
views of the Tay estuary to ogle
while dining. However, the
grandeur doesn't end here. Chef
Dominic de Franco has put his
heart into the menu – it is at once
tasty and innovative, mixing
traditional Scottish – black
pudding and haggis – with
European – wild mushroom
linguini. For both snacks and full
dinners, Bridgeview Station has
an unrivalled charm. **bridgeview-
station.com**

Bruach

■ 326 Brook Street, Broughty
Ferry, 01382 739878. Mon-Sun
10am-midnight. Food served:
Mon-Sun noon-4pm, 5-8pm

Cool purple lighting and dark
wooden panels give Bruach a
contemporary vibe. Booths and
banquettes as well as big leather
sofas make it perfect for groups,
as do the quirky copies of old
books which hide the inviting
cocktail list – a melange of
classics and modern reworkings.
The restaurant in the back serves
an ever-changing menu of
traditional fare – variations on a
steak, chicken or fish theme.

Worth visiting for a modern yet comfortable night out.

Byzantium
■ 13 Hawkhill, 01382 221946. Mon–Sun noon–3pm, 5–10pm

Reopened in late 2009, Byzantium offers an excellent choice of Mediterranean cuisine. The refurbished interior is modern and simple. The atmosphere is bustling and noisy and the food is good, as is the choice of wine. The mezze starter is highly recommended on the lunch menu, as it offers diners a few different hand-picked flavours chosen by the chef. **byzantiumrestaurant.com**

Deep Sea
■ 81 Nethergate, 01382 224449. Mon–Sat 9.30am–6.45pm

Open for coffee, snacks and, from 11.30am onwards, fish and chips, which is the thing to order here. It is a favourite place for high teas as the fish is always fresh and the chips crispy. It feels good to rest weary shopper's legs and have a civilised cuppa with the feast. The servings always come with buttered bread, the

service is friendly and the whole place unpretentious and reminiscent of a different era. Takeaway also available.

Drouthy's
■ 142 Perth Road, 01382 202187. Mon–Sun, 10am–midnight; food served: Mon–Sun, 10am–9pm

A casual and fairly studenty vibe permeates Drouthy's, which, added to its friendly staff and simple, earthy ethos, makes it a popular regular on the Dundee scene. A music venue, the basement club hosts bands of all genres, with a weekly jazz night on Sundays. Food is wholesome and inexpensive, with its Gourmet Burger a firm favourite. A big screen shows major sporting events and can also be hired for movie nights. **fullerthomson.com**

Dundee Rep Theatre Café
■ Tay Square, 01382 206699. Café bar: Mon–Sat 9.30am till late. Restaurant: Tue–Sat lunch from noon, evening meals from 5pm. Closed Sun

Venturing beyond the lobby of

◥ **Food for thought** The Dundee Rep serves up an excellent menu

this vibrant theatre is the relaxed and popular café restaurant serving Scottish/world food. The restaurant is partially closed off from the busy theatre but the buzz is there, with the upstairs bar and café area open to the comings and goings of the theatre crowd. The menu encompasses Lebanese inspired mezze starters big enough to share, steak frites and carrot cake with honey ice cream. The lunchtime soup and sandwich deal is generous and the coffee and cakes are always good. They offer a special children's menu, the wine list shows imagination and there is a good choice of other drinks.
dundeerep.co.uk

Fisherman's Tavern
■ 10-16 Fort Street, Broughty Ferry, 01382 775941. Sun–Wed, 11am-midnight; Thu–Sat, 11am-1am. Food served: Mon–Sat, noon-8pm; Sun 11am-8pm

A stone's throw from the esplanade, a row of 17th-century fisherman's cottages is now the traditional, comfy pub of today. Daily changing cask ales, local wines and award winning bar food can be enjoyed in the relative privacy of the bar's many nooks and crannies. The tavern also holds an annual charity beer festival each May, showcasing the area's beers, lagers and ales. Perfect for a relaxing drink after a riverside stroll.
fishermanstavern.co.uk

The Glass Pavilion
■ The Esplanade, Broughty Ferry, 01382 732738. Mon–Sun 10am–10pm

By far the best selling point of this impressive glass-fronted building is the location. The restaurant is a listed building, originally constructed as a bathing shelter for the adjacent beach, and still provides spectacular views over the Tay Estuary. There are several menus depending on the time and day, including a popular High Tea served daily 5–7pm.
theglasspavilion.co.uk

↘ **Heart of Glass** The Glass Pavilion is located right on the seafront

The Italian

■ 36 Commercial Street, 01382 206444. Mon-Sat: noon-2pm, Mon-Sun: dinner from 5pm

A family-run restaurant which has a gracious ambience and a selection of traditional Italian food. Pasta with rich sauces, tender steak and chicken cooked with sage, eaten from tables with starched white tablecloths. The ciabatta bread is made there and goes very well with the starters, which include such hearty fare as mozzarella and juicy tomatoes, pesto or chicken liver pâté. It has excellent seafood and provides a good value three-course set lunch. **theitalian.co.uk**

Jahangir Tandoori

■ 1 Session Street, 0871 426 5309. Mon-Sun 5pm-midnight

A luxurious entrance hall leads the way into the extravagantly decorated Jahangir Tandoori. The glamorous décor continues within: a dominating fish pond, flanked by tall, striking vases and tables lit by candlelight all add to the exotic ambiance. The authentic Pakistani, Punjabi and Bangladeshi tandoori dishes each have their own distinctive flavours and aromas, due to the fresh spices used daily. In addition to the genuine Indian recipes, a whisky twist often rears its experimental head.

Jute Café

■ Dundee Contemporary Arts, 152 Nethergate, 01382 909246. Mon-Sat 10am-midnight; Sun noon-midnight

Jute offers a bit of everything for those interested in checking out Dundee Contemporary Arts or indeed anyone just passing. A reasonably priced snack menu is available alongside a full dinner menu. Fish and vegetarian options are a big feature on the dinner menu, including a gorgeous mushroom and blue cheese risotto. Meat-eaters will find the rib-eye steak just as delicious. Quality this high is tough to find elsewhere in the city centre. **dca.org.uk/visit/jute-caf-bar.html**

Ketchup

■ 10 South Tay Street, 0845 166 6020. Sun-Thu noon-11pm; Fri & Sat noon-midnight

Relatively new to Dundee and proving very popular already, Ketchup offers a relaxed American diner atmosphere, with a menu of gourmet burgers and milkshakes. Special offers attract the nearby student population. The menu features many popular choices but, if you are feeling a bit more daring, head over to the adventurous section of the menu, where you can sample ostrich or venison burgers. Good prices and pleasant for a stress-free meal at lunch or dinner time. **socialanimal.co.uk/Dundee/Ketchup_Dundee**

↘ Get a great burger at Ketchup

Eat & Drink

↘ **Dining delight** Metro Bar and Brasserie at the Apex Hotel

Malabar
■ 304 Perth Road, 01382 646888. Mon-Sun 5pm-midnight

Malabar brings the spices of the east to Dundee in dishes influenced by southern Indian cuisine. Staff are attentive and service is fast, complementing the relaxed ambiance. Even better, the food is beautifully presented and suffused with flavour, perfectly balancing spice and fragrance in very generously sized portions. Having been around for only four years, Malabar has established its place as a welcoming restaurant with truly tasty food. **malabar-dundee.co.uk**

Mandarin Garden
■ 40-44 South Tay Street, 01382 227733. Mon-Sat noon-2pm, 6-11pm. Closed on Sun

Tucked away but close to the theatre and the DCA, this is reliable and reasonably priced, with an extensive menu featuring a few unusual items, such as lettuce dumplings, and all the usual favourites, such as Mongolian lamb and Peking duck. The seafood tends to be good, especially the steamed fish on the bone, and there is a good variety of vegetables. The atmosphere is always friendly and busy and the food arrives quickly.

Metro Bar and Brasserie
■ Apex Hotel, 1 West Victoria Dock Road, 0845 365 0002. Mon-Fri noon-2.30pm, 6-9.30pm

Part of Dundee's Apex Hotel and overlooking Victoria Dock, Metro is classy, uncluttered and bright, thanks to a wall-length window which allows for views of the gently lapping waves. A friendly welcome awaits from genial, efficient staff. The food is beautifully presented, a trait which is mirrored in taste. A starter of smooth, rich chicken parfait is complemented by a sweet plum and apple chutney, while teriyaki marinated pork is accompanied by thick egg noodles and a flavourful spicy sauce. What's more, portions are very generous and the atmosphere is relaxed, making it the perfect dockside environment to linger over a long lunch. **apexhotels.co.uk/eat**

Number Twenty Five
■ 25 South Tay Street, 0845 166 6025
socialanimal.co.uk/Dundee/ Number_Twenty_Five

See Stay, page 92

Papa Joe's
■ 15 Whitehall Street, 01382 202520. Lunch: Fri/Sat from noon, dinner: Sun–Sat 5pm–late

One of two venues (the other is in Stirling), Papa Joe's in Dundee is an enjoyable experience for families and groups. The restaurant is large, seating 140 diners and well prepared for families, with a children's menu and good changing facilities. The atmosphere is relaxed and friendly and the menu is simple yet extensive. Italian portions include steak, burgers, pasta and chicken dishes.
papa-joes.co.uk

The Parlour Café
■ 58 West Port, 01382 203588. Mon-Fri 8am-8pm; Sat 8am-5pm; Sun 10am-4pm

A small, white-fronted café sits tucked up near the university, its steamed-up windows enticing passers-by. The Parlour serves as a café and takeaway deli and holds true to its philosophy of offering healthy ingredients in mouth-watering recipes. The homemade soups and sandwiches are small bites of perfection. The popularity of the café is evident by the constant crowds at the counter and limited seating availability.

◥ Papa Joe's, in the city centre is popular with families

Eat & Drink

The Playwright

■ 11 Tay Square, 01382 223113. Mon-Sun noon-2.30pm, 5-9.30pm

Offering some of the most inventive fine dining in Dundee, with a price list to match, the Playwright aims high. It succeeds, although the grazing menu is recommended if you are on a budget. Lunch and pre-theatre also offer reasonable value at £16.95 for two courses, whereas evening à la carte can see starters fetching around £12. Head here for a very special occasion. **theplaywright.co.uk**

Rama Thai

■ 32–34 Dock Street, 01382 223366. Mon–Sun noon–2.30pm, 5–11pm

Rama Thai certainly lives up to its promise of 'fine Thai dining'. The restaurant is beautifully presented, with ornate decoration including intricate carvings on the wooden tables and chairs. The menu offers lots of choice without compromising on attention to detail and quality. There are banquet options for those who wish to try a little bit of everything and a regular menu for those familiar with Thai dining.

Robertson of Broughty Ferry

■ 234 Brook Street, Broughty Ferry, 01382 739277. Mon-Fri 9am-5pm; Sat 8.30am-5pm; Sun 11am-9pm

Robertson's is considered the Harrods of Broughty Ferry and it's easy to see why. In a packed and friendly environment baskets of goodies line the floor with shelves of jams, chutneys and vinaigrettes on the left, a deli counter on the right, and a butcher to the back. Home-grown produce is an important factor and it shows. **robertsonsbutchers.co.uk**

The Ship Inn

■ 121 Fisher Street, Broughty Ferry, 01382 779176. Restaurant open: Mon-Sat noon-3pm, 5-9.30pm; Sun 12.30-2.30pm, 5-9.30pm

The Ship Inn benefits from one of the best views in Broughty Ferry – a huge window looks out across the shingled shore and onto the Tay. The inside is based on the ward room of RRS *Discovery*, panelled wooden walls and portholes make for a nautical vibe. The menu is appropriately fish-based, with Arbroath crab and Shetland mussels fresh each day. Watch for dolphins in the summer. **theshipinn-broughtyferry.co.uk**

Speedwell Bar

■ 165-167 Perth Road, 01382 667783

Known to locals as 'Mennies', Speedwell is a listed pub which was built in 1903 and is noted for its quality interior. Etched glass, carved mahogany and glazed screens make a visit to Speedwell a lesson in architectural history as well as a trip to the pub. The staff are friendly and well trained to give advice about the 100 or more different malt whiskies. The bar also has a decent range of draught and bottled beers and a good wine selection. Worth a visit just for the décor and convenient location on the Perth Road.

Murray Chalmers
Music PR who grew up in the Lochee area of Dundee, and has worked with acts like Coldplay, Pet Shop Boys and Lily Allen.

'Dundee's music scene was a big part of my life growing up here. Dundee adopted punk – which was my thing – pretty quickly. There's still a real buzz here – anywhere that has such a brilliant art college is always going to have a strong youth culture'

Alison Campbell
Age 20

'You always have a good night out at Fat Sam's.'

Taychreggan Hotel and Restaurant
■ 4 Ellieslea Road, West Ferry, 01382 778626. **taychreggan-hotel.co.uk**

See Stay, page 93

Tea Leaves and Coffee
■ 75 Perth Road. Mon-Fri 9am-6pm, Sat 10am-6pm

At this small, adventurous café, the enthusiastic owners take great pride in serving only the most delicious drinks to their customers. These include coffee, a range of flowering teas and hot chocolate. It's very easy to spend a lazy afternoon here watching the world go by. There are newspapers to browse and homemade cakes so gooey and delicious you will probably want to eat two. For a delicious treat at lunchtime, try the deli filled rolls, which are a cut above most and it is the first place in Dundee to make green tea espresso.And, if for some reason you are avoiding caffeine, there's no need to feel left out here. The red bush tea cappuccino is satisfyingly spicy.

◥ **Tea for two** Tea Leaves and Coffee

Local Specialities

The east coast is famously fertile and rich with produce. The people here tended to preserve their food with smoke and the delicious Arbroath smokie is still made by hanging a pair of haddock over halved whisky barrels full of hot woodsmoke until they are cooked. British marmalade was invented in 18th-century Dundee when a merchant bought up a quantity of Seville oranges from a Spanish ship; when his wife found they were too bitter to eat, she cooked them with sugar, and Keiller's jam was born. Dundee cake is a feast of spices, dried fruit, lemon and almonds cooked into a traditional rich fruit cake. Nearby in Forfar, the bridie is sold as an individual pie made from shortcrust pastry and chuck steak and onion, and is still very popular today.

Trades House Bar

■ 40 Nethergate, 01382 229494. Mon-Sat 10am-midnight; Sun 11am-midnight. Food served: Mon-Sat 11am-3pm; Sun 12.30-6.30pm

A real local air infuses this lived-in, quirky bar. With stained-glass windows to splash colour among the various snugs, it is bright and airy while still retaining a cosy feel. Trades is a great place for lunch, lingering chats over coffee or a night of viewing sports, there are a large number of drinks on tap, from Tartan Special to Japanese lagers.

Twin City Café

■ 4 City Square, 01382 223662. Mon-Sat 7.30am-6pm; Sun 10.30am-4pm

The decor may be reminiscent of a seaside restaurant, all blues with white swirls and metallic railings, but Twin City Café is, instead, located in City Square at the heart of the town centre. Providing good food with a Middle Eastern twist, the café provides something different from the nearby coffee shop chains. Stuffed vine leaves and lamb and chicken kofta stand out while pasta and pizza sate the less adventurous.

Visocchi's

■ 40 Gray Street, Broughty Ferry, 01382 779297. Tue-Thu 9.30am-7pm; Sat 9.30am-8pm; Sun 9.30am-7pm. Closed Mon

Visocchi's has been a favourite with generations of locals for its staples of pasta, pizzas and ice cream. For many, a bracing walk along Broughty Ferry beach would not be complete without a trip to Visocchi's afterwards. The café restaurant has a casual atmosphere and is a popular meeting place whether you're looking for a substantial steak and salad or just a quick coffee and cake. The service is friendly, and there are usually some family members serving at the counter, where there is a constant stream of customers and great smells wafting from the kitchen.

Eat & Drink

Nightlife

Dundee has always had an excellent reputation for live music. Today's nightlife has extended beyond the smoky venues and crowded pubs and includes casinos, superclubs and even Saturday night lectures. Whatever you're in the mood for, there's bound to be some nightlife for you.

DUNDEE
ONE CITY, MANY DISCOVERIES

Art Bar

■ 140b Perth Road, 01382 227888. Mon-Sun noon-late

Across the road from the Art School, this cosy basement bar has a mixed clientele of students and professionals. The menu features snacks and bar food, and there is a wide selection of reasonably priced drinks. Live music is a feature at the weekend, and the walls are frequently adorned with the work of local artists. The atmosphere is lively and unpretentious, with welcoming bar staff on hand. Well worth a visit.

BOWIE AND THE BEATLES PLAYED THE CAIRD HALL

Caird Hall

■ City Square, 01382 434451

Caird Hall stands in the heart of Dundee overlooking City Square, a grand building renowned for its ten impressive Doric columns. Inside, the building is contemporary yet traditional, with multi-functional facilities bringing the venue up to date. From opera and comedy to pop and rock, Caird Hall has famously played host to the Beatles, Elton John and David Bowie in the past. It remains an important part of Dundee's history and cultural scene. **cairdhall.co.uk**

Nightlife

⬄ **What a performance** The Caird Hall hosts many cultural events

Public Lectures

The University of Dundee has a world-class reputation in many departments, and has found ways of reaching out to include Dundonians in academic discussion and the latest research. This policy is encapsulated in the tradition of the Saturday Evening Lecture Series which take place between January and May every year. These lectures cover a huge range of subjects from geographical exploration to psychology; they are given by experts in their field, some of whom are household names. The university also hosts the Bell Lecture Series, with respected academic speakers from the field of education. Details about the above series are available on the University of Dundee website. Another initiative by the university is

↘ Saturday night's allright for learning at University of Dundee

the café science talks, where current science issues can be discussed over a cup of coffee.
cafesciencedundee.co.uk

Chambers
■ 59-61 Gellatly Street. Open daily

Chambers is experiencing a new lease of life since starting to host gigs. The clientele has become younger, with the student population clocking on to the relaxed atmosphere and affordable drinks menu, which offers a selection of very reasonably priced beer and wine. On top of this, gigs are free. If you are interested in seeing a band, arrive a bit before the listed start time to ensure good seats, as it's a small venue.
myspace.com/ chambersbardundee

DCA
■ 152 Nethergate, 01382 909900. Mon-Sat 10am-midnight; Sun noon-midnight

The Jute Café is Dundee's home to the professional post-work drinking crowd. It reaches capacity on Friday nights between 6.30pm and 10pm so be sure to book a table or arrive early. There are plenty of cocktails and a large selection of exciting wines and beers, complemented by a lovely menu, in the restaurant and the bar area. The bar is adjacent to the DCA cinema and a large patio. **dca.org.uk**

Nightlife

Want to discover more about Dundee?

visit dundee.com

 Check out
What's On

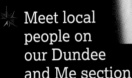 Meet local
people on
our Dundee
and Me section

Find out more about what Dundonians
think of their city

Learn about our innovators and
ambassadors

Get further details of what to do here
and where to stay.

Read the latest news from the city

Its all on dundee.com

DUNDEE
ONE CITY, MANY DISCOVERIES

The Doghouse
■ 15 Ward Street, 01382 206812

The Doghouse has recently moved and is now housed in a converted church. Despite its new location, the regulars have remained faithful, providing a buzzing atmosphere. This establishment prides itself on hosting less mainstream acts than the nearby Fat Sam's. The MySpace page is packed with information on all of the upcoming events, and seldom does a night go by without a performance. Open Mic Night comes highly recommended.
myspace.com/dundeedoghouse

↘ **Sing a song** Great music at Duke's Corner

Duke's Corner
■ 13 Brown Street, 01382 205052.
Mon-Sun noon-midnight

An impressive building with a large beer garden, Duke's is situated in the old Doghouse building. In keeping with the previous tenants, Duke's is a live music venue and hosts an array of gigs and comedy nights. The interior has been smartened up with two areas – the main bar and the performance area. The Duke's Corner is a popular choice for a more unique night out with its laid-back, jazz club-style set-up and a wide selection of beers on offer.
myspace.com/dukescorner

Kyle Falconer and Kieren Webster
The View is an indie rock band from Dryburgh in Dundee. Kyle Falconer, lead singer, Peter Reilly, guitarist, Kieren Webster, bassist and Steven Morrison, drummer were all born and grew up in the city. theviewareonfire. com

'Dundee is alive with loads of great young talent. Great bands are coming out of the city and it's a fantastic social thing for young people to have. Music venues are springing up all over Dundee, like Duke's Corner. It was sad to see the old Doghouse close as that was our old stomping ground, but the new venue is pretty cool too.'

↘ **Only the best** The VIP room in Fat Sams is a very popular haunt

Fat Sam's
■ 31 South Ward Road, 01382 228181

One of Dundee's top gig and comedy venues, Fat Sam's mixes established and popular bands with newer, more edgy local-bred music. It is also the Dundee home of Just Laugh, who put on comedy nights around Central Scotland. The impressive listings are available on its website. There is a mixture of customers, depending on what is showing, and though not intimate, the atmosphere is relaxed and friendly. **fatsams.co.uk**

G Casino
■ 142 West Marketgait, 01382 309120. Open 24 hours.

Dundee's newest casino, G Casino is a slick operation; the all-day license means it can cater for revellers whatever the time of day. As well as the gaming areas, G offers a modern restaurant and elegant bar, often with entertainment. The well-designed interior and extensive drinks list makes this a venue for a trendy crowd, whether they're playing the tables or not. **gcasino.co.uk/dundee**

Liquid and Envy
■ 21 South Ward Road, 0845 313 2584. Wed, Fri & Sat 10.30pm–2.30am

Dundee's newest club offers a twin clubbing experience. One entry fee gains access to two different scenes. Giant screens surround the dance floor in Liquid as chart music is pumped from the speakers. Envy has more themed music nights such as '80s, '90s or R'n'B. The crowd is young (and sometimes in fancy dress) and drinks are generally cheap.
liquidclubs.com/dundee

London Nightclub
■ 4 Meadowside, 01382 909192. Mon–Sun 10.30pm–2.30am

Popular with locals, London caters for clubbers of all ages, from teenagers with white trainers to hen nights. The four rooms each offer a different sound, from commercial music in room one to classics and anthems in the piano bar. The club hosts foam parties and is Dundee's home to the popular 'Glam' nights. Expect a night of strobe lighting and silliness. **london-nightclub.com**

Mono
■ Airlie Place, 01382 386003

Dundee's award winning Student Union houses this club. Home to 'Skint', which claims to be the cheapest club night in Dundee, Mono also hosts the odd gem in the form of University Society fundraisers. These include themed nights, which always attract a rowdy but friendly clientele. On closing, a hotdog stand appears in typical student style. Head to Mono for a cheap and cheerful night out, and don't forget your student ID. **dusa.co.uk**

⬎ **A degree in dancing** You don't need lots of money for a night out at Mono

Ged Grimes
Ged runs Jack's Hoose Music, whose core business is creating music soundtracks for the global computer games industry. Dundee born and bred, Ged returned to the city after living in Spain.

'Dundee's music scene is as good as ever. The city has definitely changed over recent years but there's still such an eclectic and fantastic mix of music here – from great dance music and DJs right through to top singer/songwriting talent and traditional folk music. I think the city is of a size that allows people to grow at their own pace. Dundee has a great record for producing musical talent.'

Nightlife

Martel Maxwell
Martel is a freelance journalist and columnist. Her debut novel, *Scandalous* is set in Dundee.

'We're not just on the map, we are shaping the music scene in Scotland and the UK.'

Gavin McDonald
Age 19

'Dundee is brilliant for a night out – the new Casino is a great addition.'

Gema Johnsen
Age 21

'Dundee has a great student community with brilliant nightlife. Its size is perfect because the city is easy to navigate around and has everything you need.'

Out Nightclub
■ 124 Seagate. Wed–Sun, 11pm-2.30am

The only gay nightclub in Dundee, Out is defined by all accounts as a really great night out. Fresh and fun, each night has a different theme, from Wicked Wednesday to Chill Out Sunday, with Freak Out Friday starting the weekend off with a bang. Music comes courtesy of the three DJs, who take requests and really know how to get the party started. Cheap entry and drinks promos each night mean it won't break the bank.

The Phoenix
■ 103 Nethergate, 01382 200014. Mon–Sun 11am–midnight

A small, shabby-looking pub on this busy street has been open for about 150 years. All the more endearing for its scuffed edges, locals and students congregate here together under the stained-glass window. With an excellent choice of ales and beers, the Phoenix gets very busy at weekends. It's likely to be around for another 100 years.

The Reading Rooms
■ Blackscroft, 01382 228496 (enquiries made through Groucho's)

The Reading Rooms has established itself as an alternative, chilled out club, hosting a sparkling array of DJs in its quirky building, an old schoolhouse. Drinks are moderately priced, with friendly bar and door staff. The atmosphere is more relaxed than many other clubs in Dundee, and the clientele are generally very friendly. It has recently hosted acts as diverse as Mr Scruff and Jazzy Jeff. Head here for the DJ nights and you won't be disappointed.
myspace.com/thereadingrooms

Tonic
■ 141 Nethergate, 01382 226103

Located right in the middle of Dundee's student area, Tonic's main clientele are students of all ages. Its menu is affordable,

⬂ **Going underground** Head for a night of DJ fun at Underground

offering deals on cocktails, coffee and beer. It prides itself on a huge burger menu, which is a novelty if you feel hunger pangs while out for a drink. It is quite a small bar, lovely on a week night when you can hear yourself think, more difficult at weekends when it fills to bursting.

Underground
■ 25 South Tay Street, 0845 166 6025

Hidden away on the edge of the university area, Underground frequently hosts student nights, as well as special DJ nights. The DJ nights can either feature their resident acts or, less frequently, special guests. Prices depend on which night it is, although generally they are very reasonable. Entry fee

and clientele vary depending on the event, so it's best to check what is on before heading down.

The Westport Bar
■ 66 North Lindsay Street, 01382 200008

TONIC IS QUITE A SMALL BAR, LOVELY ON A WEEK NIGHT

Located close to many of Dundee's nightclubs, for some people the Westie may just be a place to stop for a quick pint. However, the bar has its own charm and an excellent reputation for live music and new bands. Previous names to grace the stage in the live venue area include Paolo Nutini as well as local bands. A mix of old man's pub and young man's playground makes the Westport an ideal visit.

Stay

Rest your weary head in some of Dundee's best places to stay. Global chains, luxury independents or refurbished hostels, Dundee offers a range of accommodation to suit everyone's tastes and pockets.

DUNDEE
ONE CITY, MANY DISCOVERIES

⬂ **Docking station** The Apex has stunning views over the quayside

Apex Dundee City Quay and Spa
◼ 1 West Victoria Dock Road, 01382 202404

The luxury choice for accommodation in Dundee, the Apex Hotel is located in Dundee's City Quay, close to all local amenities. The design was the result of an ambitious art project, hence the striking exterior. Inside, the hotel offers modern facilities in a relaxing atmosphere. Metro, the restaurant and bar, has an excellent reputation (page 70) and is frequently visited by locals as well as hotel guests. A glass wall provides an abundance of light to the dining area, offering a view of the calm waters of the City Quay. Prices can start as low as £64.
apexhotels.co.uk

Discovery Quay Premier Inn
◼ Riverside Drive, 08701 977 079

This riverside hotel is only a hop and a skip away from Dundee's famous Discovery Point. Simple rooms and reasonable prices make a stay in this hotel pleasant and unpretentious and the staff are friendly – always a bonus. City centre restaurants and pubs are within a short walking distance and there are beautiful riverside views right on the hotel's doorstep. There are two other Premier Inns, one on the outskirts of the city, and one in Broughty Ferry.
premierinn.com

Dundee Carlton Hotel
◼ 2 Dalgleish Road, 01382 462056

With only nine bedrooms, the Carlton adds a personal touch to your stay. The hotel has excellent views over the river and the recently refurbished rooms are clean and spacious, offering family accommodation as well as double rooms. The staff are helpful and the breakfast is well reputed.
dundeecarlton.com

Stay

↘ The nautical Fisherman's Tavern

Fisherman's Tavern
■ 10-16 Fort Street, Broughty Ferry, 01382 775941

In the heart of Broughty Ferry, with excellent transport links to Dundee, the Fisherman's Tavern is housed in some old fishing cottages a few seconds' walk from the Tay. An award-winning bar is downstairs, usually filled with a host of regulars. The rooms have recently been refurbished, most of them are ensuite and a Scottish breakfast is included. A little gem away from the bustle of the city.
fishermanstavern.co.uk

Hilton Dundee
■ Earl Grey Place, 01382 229271

A large hotel near to the city centre, the Hilton Dundee features all the services you associate with an international hotel group, such as a swimming pool, room service and decent rooms. The great location means the central entertainment zone is within easy walking distance. Additionally, the hotel restaurant offers some fabulous views of the river. A popular choice with many visitors, especially for those travelling on business, the Hilton Dundee offers the reliable service that has made its name across the world.
hilton.co.uk/dundee

↘ **Head to bed** The Hilton Dundee is excellently placed for the city

↘ **Happy Hoppo** Dundee's High Street hostel has been refurbished

Holiday Inn Express
■ 41 Dock Street, 01382 314330

The Holiday Inn Express is a popular choice for business travel, due to its central location. Friendly staff and a glass-walled bar and breakfast area makes a visit to the hotel a fresh and inviting experience. Being an express hotel, bathroom facilities stretch to showers only (no baths), but the rooms are adequate, and the doubles also contain a sofa for a third person. There's no restaurant but a continental breakfast is complimentary. Prices typically start at £84 but can be less during quieter periods. **holidayinnexpress-dundee.com**

Hoppo Hostel
■ 71 High Street, 01382 224646

The clichéd image of a dingy hostel could not be further from the truth at Hoppo. The magnificently restored building hosts a mixture of single, double and multi rooms – all with secure electronic key access. Excellently located right in the middle of the pedestrian precinct of the city centre, the Hoppo Hostel boasts several communal areas for meeting new friends including a guest kitchen, dining room, common room – with satellite TV – and pool room. Bedrooms are clean, and some have ensuite facilities. Amenities include free linen, towel hire and internet access.The reception is open from 8am to midnight and there is no curfew for late owls. Hoppo is a suitable stay for individuals and groups alike and the staff are always on hand to help out.
hoppo.com/dundee

THE HOSTEL BOASTS SEVERAL COMMUNAL AREAS

Hotel Broughty Ferry
■ 16 West Queen Street, Broughty Ferry, 01382 480027

On the road into Broughty Ferry sits this little hotel. The rooms are of a high standard, clean, comfortable and well looked after. It is a short walk from the centre of Broughty Ferry and the beach on the banks of the Tay. The restaurant serves simple but tasty food and the included breakfast is very good. A swimming pool, sauna and solarium provide a relaxing break before heading to the bar. The friendly staff will do their utmost to help you.
hotelbroughtyferry.co.uk

Invercarse
■ 371 Perth Road, 01382 669231

Located on the Perth Road, near Dundee's cultural heart, the Invercarse Hotel manages to escape the noisy bustle of the city centre while still being within walking distance of all attractions and local amenities. Set back from the road via a

↘ Friendly service and great views at Hotel Broughty Ferry

leafy driveway, this Best Western hotel offers a homely visit with good facilities amid slightly dated décor. Perfect for a slower-paced visit to the city. Prices for a double room start at £89.
bw-invercarsehotel.co.uk

Landmark
■ Kingsway West, 01382 641122

The Landmark has undergone a massive refurbishment, transforming it into a luxury hotel in grounds away from the road. You can expect a good standard of service within the tastefully decorated hotel, with the usual features of a restaurant and bar, room service and TV/Wi-Fi. There is also a well-equipped leisure centre and pool. The hotel is a short distance from the city centre, in a good position for travel from the A90 and great for those with their own transport.
thelandmarkdundee.co.uk

↘ Luxury at the Landmark

Stay

Lesley Riddoch
Writer, commentator and broadcaster

'Dundee is a very playful city. It's physically inspiring; the people are the funniest in Scotland. It's slightly lateral and down to earth all mixed together.'

Clive Gillman
Director, Dundee Contemporary Arts

'Over the past decade Dundee has made great strides in being recognised as a leading player in the cultural life of Scotland, reinventing itself as a centre of contemporary culture in all its forms and building towards a future in which a sense of cultural ambition informs all it does.'

Number Twenty Five
■ 25 South Tay Street, 0845 166 6025

A popular venue for dining and drinking, Number Twenty Five also offers boutique hotel facilities. Located on a popular street for city wining and dining, the four top-floor rooms are individually decorated to create a unique and personalised experience for guests. The venue offers a ground floor bar and dining area, upstairs restaurant and is located above the Underground club (page 85) – an alternative to the mainstream clubs in town. Perfect for a romantic getaway or an extra special visit.
socialanimal.co.uk/Dundee/ Number_Twenty_Five

❧ **Dundee expects** The large Queen's hotel

Queen's Hotel
■ 160 Nethergate, 01382 322515

Built in 1878, the Queen's Hotel is a huge building situated at the top of the Perth Road, close to the DCA and other bars, restaurants and attractions. It may have a slightly dated interior, but the hotel still has a decent reputation and offers the usual facilities found in a Best Western hotel, including free Wi-Fi. As well as the hotel's own restaurant, the choice of places to dine in the area is abundant. You'll be in good company – Sir Winston Churchill used the hotel as a base for his successful 1908 election campaign.
queenshotel-dundee.com

↘ **Country house living** Woodlands Hotel offers excellent facilities

Taychreggan Hotel
■ 4 Ellieslea Road, West Ferry, 01382 778626

Dating back to 1876, Taychreggan was once a private house and the ten-bedroom hotel is still privately owned. Offering some excellent river views, the hotel is also renowned for its beautiful garden, which can be appreciated from the sun terrace. In addition to the restaurant, the award-winning bar stocks more than 400 single malt whiskies and a good wine list. The location is also great, within close proximity to both Dundee and Broughty Ferry.
taychreggan-hotel.co.uk

Travelodge
■ 152-158 West Marketgait, 0871 984 6301

A budget option if you book early, Travelodge has deals that can begin as low as £19. This branch gets busy at weekends, in large part due to its location near to the big nightclubs. While it may not be the most attractive building in the city, this hotel is in a great location, making it an excellent choice for an overnight excursion to Dundee. Rooms include a TV and offer a pay-for-use Wi-Fi service.
travelodge.co.uk

Woodlands Hotel
■ 13 Panmure Terrace, Broughty Ferry, 01382 480033

The Woodlands is a small, intimate hotel, situated out of Dundee, but very near to Broughty Ferry. It is relaxed, with a friendly bar and smart restaurant. Reception staff are very helpful, and the rooms are clean and comfortable. There is a small leisure club in the hotel, housing a pool, gym, steam room and sauna. Book early to take advantage of good deals.
bw-woodlandshotel.co.uk

Stay

Explore

Ideally located in the heart of the country, Dundee is a great base for anyone looking to explore the best of what Scotland has to offer. From mountain climbing to sand yachting, Pictish trails or Peter Pan, there's a wealth of exciting things to do within a short distance of the city centre.

DUNDEE
ONE CITY, MANY DISCOVERIES

Angus Pictish Trail

■ The trail leaflet can be picked up at Pictavia Visitor Centre, Brechin, 01356 623050. Mon-Sat 9am-5pm; Sun 10am-5pm. Admission £3.25 adult. The stones are freely accessible in the landscape or preserved in small museums open between Apr-Sep. Check the website for access details. The trail can also be downloaded from pictavia.org.uk

The Picts lived in what is now north east Scotland around 2000 years ago. The impressive carved stones that can be seen on this trail were probably memorial stones, carved with heraldic symbols, beasts and scenes from important events such as the Battle of Dunnichen in 685. After conversion to Christianity the Pictish stone-masons added elaborate crosses to their repertoire. The trail takes up to four days; a visit to Pictavia, an interpretive centre, gives the context. Highlights include the sculptured stones at Aberlemno, in the Meffan Institute, St Vigean's and Meigle Museums.

Arbroath Abbey

■ Abbey Street, Arbroath, 01241 878756. Apr-Sep: Mon-Sun 9.30am-5.30pm; Oct-Mar: 9.30am-4.30pm. Admission £4.70

The sandstone ruins are a magnificent landmark in this coastal town. The abbey was founded in 1178 by William the Lion and built as a memorial to Thomas Becket. It is famous for the 1320 Declaration of Arbroath when the earls and barons of Scotland wrote to the pope affirming their independence from England and their allegiance to Robert the Bruce. The abbey ruins are impressive, especially the church façade and Abbot's House, and the visitor centre is packed with historical displays. **historic-scotland.gov.uk**

Brechin Castle Centre

■ Haughmuir, Brechin, 01356 626813. Mon-Fri 9am-5pm (6pm summer only), Sat 9am-6pm, Sun 10am-6pm. Admission to country park £3.50

This large retail centre selling plants, food and gifts, linen and books, also has an exciting play area in a country park with an ornamental lake, nature trails,

↘ One of the Pictish standing stones at Aberlemno

⬎ **Plain sailing** Brechin Castle Centre has a fine ornamental pond

model farm and a restaurant serving home baking. The landscaping has still to mature but there is something to suit the whole family here. The centre is beside Pictavia, a visitor attraction that tells the story of the Picts.
brechincastlecentre.co.uk

Caledonian Steam Railway
■ The Station, Park Road, Brechin. 01356 622992. Jun & Sep: Sun; Jul & Aug: Sat & Sun. Admission varies

A group of volunteers run summer weekend train rides from here for four miles into the Angus countryside to the Bridge of Dun station. Within walking distance is the House of Dun, an 18th-century house and gardens open to the public. Specials offers run throughout the year.
caledonianrailway.co.uk

Glamis Castle
■ 01307 840393, 15 Mar-Oct: 10am-6pm, Nov-31 Dec: 10.30am-4.30pm. Closed Dec 24-26. Admission £6 (adult)

This is one of Scotland's must-see destinations. Just to go down the straight oak-lined avenue with the castle at the end is a spectacular experience. The supposedly haunted building, where HM Queen Elizabeth, the Queen Mother, grew up, is steeped in history and filled with wonderful furniture, tapestry, china and pictures. You can get freshly cooked food in the Victorian kitchen restaurant and pick up souvenirs in the gift shop outside. Leave time to walk around the Italian garden and parklands planted with superb mature trees. The 17th-century monumental sundial in the grounds is worth a special detour and, if you have

THE GARDENS OF THE CASTLE DATE FROM THE 18TH CENTURY

John O'Rourke

Publisher and MD of Clash Magazine. John runs the Dundee-based *Clash Magazine*, an award-winning publication, as well as www.clash music.com.

'Dundee has so many positives. You've got the city life but it's also so easy to connect to the outdoors, the beaches, the countryside. There's also the fact it gets more hours of sunshine than any other city in Scotland.'

Nick Wright
Age 42

'On the edge of the North Sea, the highlands and the central belt, not urban alone, nor rural – Dundee is simply a brilliant place.'

children with you, they'll want a shot on the playground and a look at the highland cattle. At the village end of one of the avenues, close to the village church, is the ancient St Fergus's Well. If you walk there, take a look at the Pictish stone and then peek into the cottage museum about Angus folklore. The castle and grounds host a variety of events, including a classical music prom, highland games and a country-side festival. **glamis-castle.co.uk**

↘ **By royal command** Glamorous Glamis

Glendoick Garden Centre and Restaurant
■ A90 Perth-Dundee Road, 01738 860260, Mon-Sat 9am-5pm, Sun 10am-5pm (slightly longer hours in the summer). Closed 25 & 26 Dec, 31 Dec-4 Jan

This garden centre is owned by the Cox family, Dundee jute manufacturers who turned plantsmen, famous for their plant-hunting expeditions over three generations. Check out the website for their private garden openings. The family sell specialist azaleas and rhododendrons, many bred by them. The centre also sells food and every-thing for the garden, with the emphasis on hardy plants suitable for the Scottish climate. There is a café and an attractive display garden where you can see the plants growing before you buy. **glendoick.com**

Explore

Glenshee
■ Cairnwell Pass, 013397 41320

The glen of fairies is a beautiful place in all seasons. Known for its walking in the summer and for great skiing in the winter, it is about one hour's drive from Dundee. When the snow is good and the wind factor is not too strong you can imagine yourself in the Alps. Facilities are basic, but ski hire is easily arranged, as are lessons in snowsports. There is 40 km of marked piste, with plenty of scope for the intermediate skier/snowboarder on the twenty-six blue and red runs and two exciting black runs for the skilful. Beginners are also well looked after with nursery slopes and green runs. The surrounding hills are wonderful to walk in at all times of the year, with a Corbett (2500ft high) mountain, Ben Gulabin, approached from Spittal of Glenshee. **ski-glenshee.co.uk**

Golf

The golf courses of Dundee have always had to live in the shadow of their more famous neighbouring courses, but within the city environs are six courses that merit the attention of any golfer. The council owns and runs Caird Park and Camperdown, both offering very affordable golf to all. Camperdown especially is one of the better undiscovered parkland courses of Scotland and deserves much wider recognition. Downfield is an Open Championship qualifying course and one of the best inland courses you will find. Ballumbie Castle and Piperdam are both

↘ Glorious greens at Downfield

relatively new parkland-type courses based around housing developments and they both offer a good test for golfers of all abilities. Monifieth is the nearest of the famed stretch of Angus links courses to Dundee and offers two 18-hole courses. The Medal course is another Open Championship qualifying course and Carnoustie plays regular host to The Open.

■ **Ballumbie Castle**, Old Quarry Road, Off Ballumbie Road, 01382 730026, ballumbiecastle golfclub.com/
■ **Caird Park**, Mains Loan, 01382 438871, dundeecity.gov .uk/golf/main.htm
■ **Camperdown Country Park**, Coupar Angus Road, 01382 431820, dundeecity.gov.uk/golf/ main.htm
■ **Carnoustie Country** carnoustiecountry.com
■ **Downfield**, Turnberry Avenue, 01382 825595, downfieldgolf.co.uk/
■ **Monifieth Golf Links**, Monifieth Links, Princes Street, Monifieth, 01382 532767, monifiethgolf.co.uk
■ **Piperdam Golf & Leisure Resort**, Fowlis, 01382 581374, piperdam.com/

Explore

JM Barrie's Birthplace
■ 9 Brechin Road, Kirriemuir,
01575 572646/0844 4392142.
Opening times vary, call for
details. Admission £5.50

Barrie, creator of Peter Pan and
one of ten children, was born in
this charming 19th-century two-
storey cottage in 1860. That the
family lived modestly is
reflected in the furnishings. No
11 is fitted out as an exhibition
space where you can see
manuscripts and theatrical
costumes worn in the stage
productions of *Peter Pan*.
Outside, willow is fashioned into
a crocodile. Pirate workshops
take place, with children
enjoying crafts and games.

Land Yachting
■ West Sands, St Andrews,
07784 121125

Land yachting, a relatively new
sport, is available on beaches
near to Arbroath and St

Andrews. The year-round
activities offered by local
business Blown Away include
special family days, childrens'
sports and even stag and hen
parties. It also offers kayaking,
and occasionally 'beach
Olympics' competitions. An
action-packed day out with
family or friends.
blownawaylandyachts.co.uk

Lunan Bay
■ Inverkeilor

The beach of choice for many
Dundonians is about forty
minutes in the car. This is a place
to walk for hours, or surf, or
swim. The sand is pale and fine
though studded in parts with
gloriously coloured pebbles.
When the tide is very high, it is
possible to walk along the top of
the sand dunes. The southern end
of the beach leads to a coastal
path which meanders for about
seven miles, ending in
Auchmithie and taking you

Cycling

The Green Circular is an illu-
minating route that
encompasses the whole of the
city and its outskirts. Designed
as a way to see parts of the city
you wouldn't discover
otherwise, it has been devised
to include as few roads as
possible, so is very family
friendly and safe for all ages
and for the less experienced
cyclist. The east section leaves
central Dundee via the old
docks and heads towards
Broughty Ferry, with beautiful
Tay views along the way. It
passes through a quaint

nature reserve and into Monifieth. It doubles back around
the green northern areas of the
city before passing around
Ninewells Hospital and
heading back into the centre. If
you want to tackle only a part
of it, go for the Dundee to
Broughty Ferry path: the views
are unrivalled.

Explore

⬂ **Wide open spaces** Life's a beach at Lunan Bay

excitingly close to the sandstone cliffs. In the nesting season, you can see puffins on the cliff edges and, looking inland, see the hills of Angus rising beyond the cultivated fields.

Perth Racecourse
■ Scone Palace Park, Perth, 01738 551597 (Ticket Hotline). Season runs from Apr-Sep

If you've never had a trip to the races, then Perth Racecourse is the perfect place to start. This award-winning course is considered to be a good testing ground for the bigger races later in the season. City of Perth Gold Cup Day, held in late May, is one of the biggest events here, usually attracting over 11,000 spectators. **perth-races.co.uk**

Scone Palace
■ Perth, 01738 552300. Apr-Oct: Mon-Fri & Sun

9.30am-5pm; Sat 9.30am-4pm. Closed Nov-Mar. Admission £9 (Adult)

Once the place where the Kings of Scotland were crowned, and rightful home to the Stone of Destiny (now in Edinburgh Castle), Scone Palace is a vital key in understanding the history of the country. Situated just outside Perth, Scone Palace is still a family home (to the Earls of Mansfield), and an extremely popular visitor attraction. As well as touring the Palace and the splendid grounds, there are often events taking place here, from the Scottish Game Fair to International Horse Trials. **scone-palace.co.uk**

St Andrews
■ Fife

Old and new blends together in this ancient university town where the buildings date from as

the mcmanus

DUNDEE'S ART GALLERY & MUSEUM

Now open to the public

Mon to Sat 10am - 5pm
Sun 12.30 - 4.30pm
Last entry is 15 minutes
before gallery closing time

Admission Free

The McManus:
Dundee's Art Gallery & Museum
Albert Square
Meadowside
Dundee
DD1 1DA

For further information on how to find
McManus, events and facilities please
visit the website or call **01382 307200**.

RECOGNISED

The City's fine art, decorative
art and whaling collections are
recognised as being of national
significance.

www.themcmanus-dundee.gov.uk

HISTORIC SCOTLAND

PROJECT PART-FINANCED
BY THE EUROPEAN UNION

Europe and Scotland
Making it **work together**

early as the 13th century. Legend says the relics of St Andrew were brought here by St Rule, some time before golf was invented here in the 15th century. The beach and the golf courses make it a great place for a holiday, while the closes and streets are fun to explore. As well as the 12th-century Cathedral ruins, the town has quality boutiques, food shops, cafés and restaurants and caters well for cultural interests. There is a theatre, cinema and museum, and the galleries include the Fraser Gallery for contemporary Scottish art.

Tentsmuir Nature Reserve and Beach
■ 01382 553704

Across the Tay Bridge, a mile and a half from Tayport, this nature reserve has a stunning beach, forest walks, wild-fowling hides by three fresh-water lochs and a species-rich dune heath. You can walk from Tayport or approach it from the Forestry Commission car park off the B945. The butterflies, flowers, birds and seals are in their element here and the beach is in a constant state of flux as it

↘ Tentsmuir Nature Reserve

is moulded by the Tay and the tides. **tentsmuir.org**

Wind surfing
■ Monikie Country Park, 01382 370202. May-Sep

In the beautiful Monikie Country Park, Adventure Scotland provides both windsurfing taster sessions and more serious training. The sessions run in the summer months with tasters usually held in the evenings. The instructors are fully trained and offer encouragement to beginners of all ages. The park also offers kayaking, trout fishing, a locally famous adventure playground and Byzantium (page 67) run a café here.
adventure.visitscotland.com

The Angus Glens

From Dundee it is 17 miles to Kirriemuir where the landscape changes to wild moorland and hills. There are six main glens; Prosen, Ogil, Lethnott, Isla, Clova and Esk. They all include rivers or burns with grassland, livestock and birch trees alongside, rising to heather. There is very good walking in all the glens with a number of Munros (mountains over 3000ft) easily reached and several marked paths, such as Jock's Road from Glen Clova to Braemar. A walking festival is held every June, with walks led by rangers.
angusahead.com/ walkingfestival

Explore

Information

Dundee is in a great location for visitors from all over Scotland, the UK and the rest of the world. Easy to get to from Edinburgh, Glasgow and Aberdeen, this section will tell you how to get there how to get around, and provide you with all the information you'll need for a great trip.

DUNDEE
ONE CITY, MANY DISCOVERIES

Travel & useful contacts

Air
■ Dundee Airport (DDE),
Riverside, 01382 662200

Dundee is well-served by a small
but very convenient airport, located
just beside the Tay.
Scheduled flights leave from here
for London City, Belfast City,
Birmingham and Jersey in the
summer, and some chartered
package holidays depart from here
too – contact airlines and tour
operators for timetable information
(see website for details). The
terminal has a small café, and both
long and short stay car parks.
The rail and bus stations are only a
five-minute drive from the airport,
taking the stress out of connecting
journeys. While there are always
taxis waiting, a bus service into the
city centre operates too.
hial.co.uk/dundee-airport.html

Car Hire
■ **Arnold Clark**, East Dock Street,
01382 225382,
arnoldclarkrental.com
■ **Europcar**, 45-53 Gellatly
Street, 01382 455505,
europcar.co.uk
■ **Sixt**, 18 Marketgait, 0844
4993399, sixt.co.uk
■ **Thrifty Car & Van Rental**,
Kingsway Park, 01382 621169,
thrifty.co.uk

Coach & Bus
■ Dundee Bus Station, Seagate,
0871 200 2233 (Travel Line)
01382 614550 (other enquiries)

Dundee is well-served by
crosscountry coaches, and
National Express, Megabus and
Stagecoach operate services to
and through the city. National

↘ Dundee Airport has great links
and is convenient for the city centre

Express also operates within the
city itself, offering Day Saver
tickets, which are handy for
covering a lot of gound in one
day. See individual company
websites for more details.
**nationalexpress.com,
traveldundee.co.uk,
megabus.com/uk,
stagecoachbus.com**

Cycle Hire
■ **Spokes**, 272 Perth Road, 01382
666644, spokescycles.net

General information
For more information on, and to
sign up for regular newsletters
about Dundee, One City, Many
Discoveries, see the new website,
dundee.com

Newspapers
■ **The Courier**
Mon-Sat, thecourier.co.uk

■ Evening Telegraph
Mon–Fri, eveningtelegraph.co.uk

NHS 24
■ 08454 242424, nhs24.com

NHS Tayside
■ 01382 818 479 (office number)

Ninewells Hospital
■ Ninewells Avenue, 01382 660111, nhstayside.scot.nhs.uk

Pedal & Foot
One of the best things about a compact city centre is the ability to get around under your own steam. The Dundee Travel Info website has information on cycling routes as well as a handy walk planner.
dundeetravelinfo.com, dundee-travelactive.com

Road
Dundee is well-connected to the rest of the UK, being on the A90 from Glasgow and Edinburgh to Aberdeen. There is also a scenic route from Edinburgh through Fife and into Dundee over the Tay Road Bridge.

Tayside Police
■ West Bell Street, 0300 111 2222 (non-emergency number), 01382 591591 (lost & found property). Call 999 or 112 in an emergency. tayside.police.uk

Taxis
■ **Dundee 50 50 50**, 01382 505050
■ **Dundee Private Hire**, 01382 203020, dundeecabs.com
■ **Skycabs Direct**, 01382 500555, dundeetaxis.com
■ **Tay Taxis**, 01382 450450, tay-taxis.co.uk
■ **Tele-Taxis** 01382 669333

Train
■ Dundee Railway Station (DEE), South Union Street, 08457 48 49 50 (National Rail Enquiries)

Again, the city benefits from excellent rail links as it is on both the Edinburgh and Glasgow main-line to Aberdeen. The station is within walking distance of most of the city centre. Check the Trainline and National Rail websites for timetables.
nationalrail.co.uk, thetrainline.com

Tourist Information
■ VisitScotland Information Centre, Discovery Point, 01382 527527

Dundee's main tourist infomation centre is handily located at Discovery Point, and staff there will be happy to help with all aspects of your stay.
angusanddundee.co.uk

City centre map

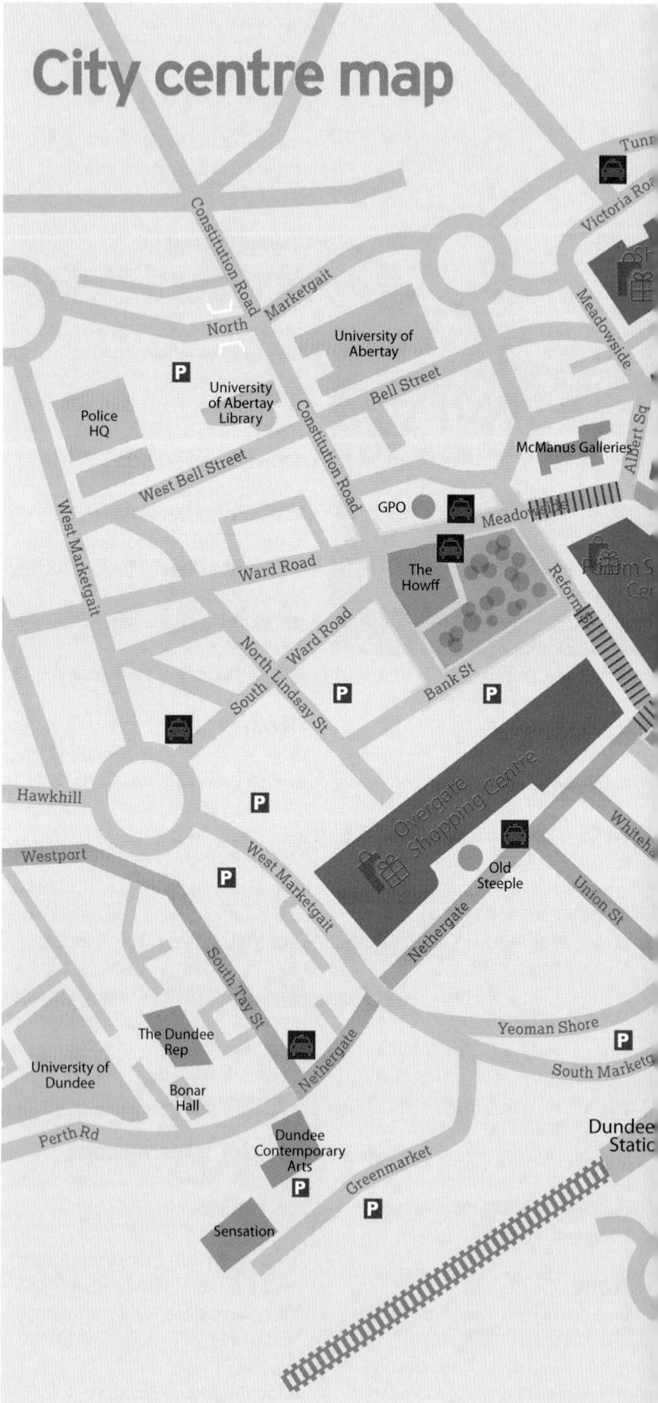

Tunn
Victoria Roa

Constitution Road

Marketgait

North

University of
Abertay

Bell Street

P

University
of Abertay
Library

Police
HQ

Meadowside

Albert Sq

McManus Galleries

West Bell Street

Constitution Road

GPO

Meado

West Marketgait

Ward Road

The
Howff

Reform

North Lindsay St

Ward Road

Bank St

P

P

South Lindsay St

P

Hawkhill

P

Overgate
Shopping Centre

West Marketgait

Westport

Old
Steeple

Union St

Whiteha

Nethergate

South Tay St

Yeoman Shore

The Dundee
Rep

Nethergate

South Market

P

University of
Dundee

Bonar
Hall

Perth Rd

Dundee
Contemporary
Arts

Greenmarket

Dundee
Static

P

P

Sensation

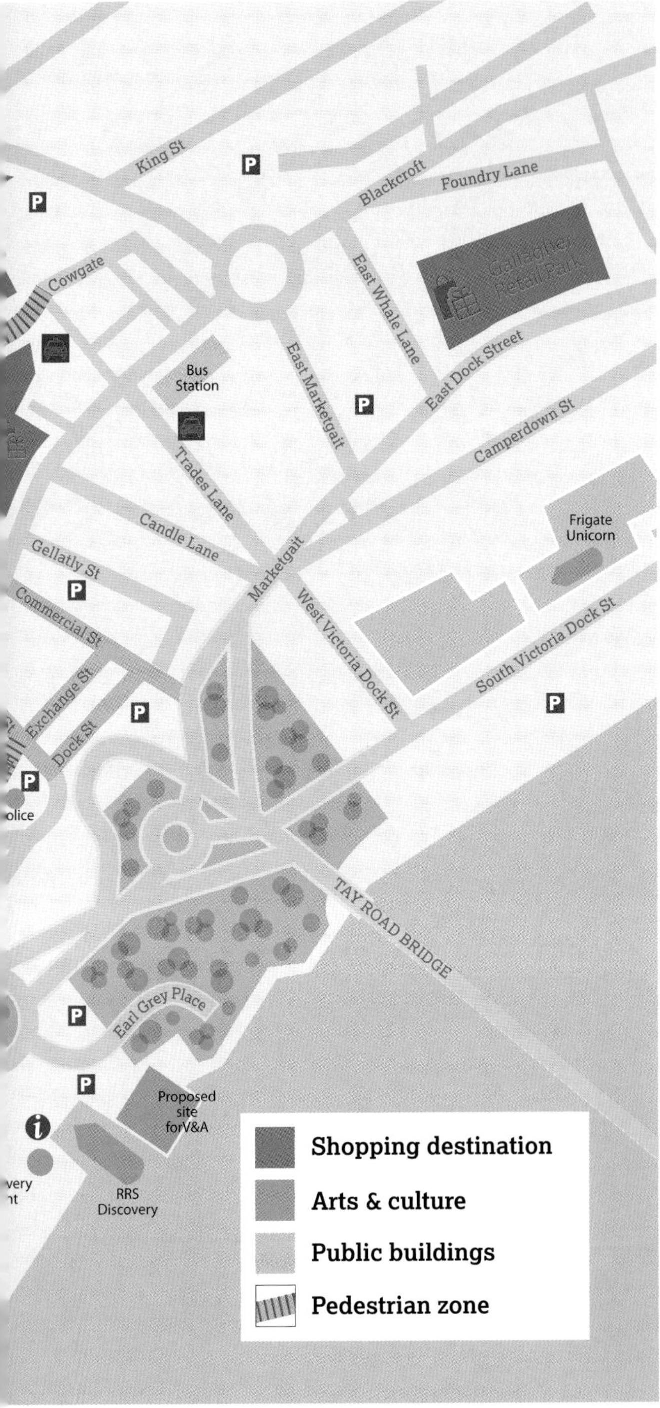

King St

Blackcroft

Foundry Lane

Cowgate

East Whale Lane

East Dock Street

Gallagher
Retail Park

Bus
Station

East Marketgait

Camperdown St

Trades Lane

Candle Lane

Gellatly St

Markgait

Frigate
Unicorn

Commercial St

West Victoria Dock St

Exchange St

South Victoria Dock St

Dock St

olice

TAY ROAD BRIDGE

Earl Grey Place

Proposed
site
for V&A

very
nt

RRS
Discovery

Shopping destination

Arts & culture

Public buildings

Pedestrian zone

MEALL REAMHAR ▲ 565
1069 ▲
975 ▲ CARN LIATH
903 ▲ BEN VUIRICH
Spittal of Glenshee
▲ MONAMEANOCH
B8079 Blair Atholl
BEN VRACKIE ▲ 841
Straloch
740 ▲ BADANDUN HILL
Killiekrankie
A924
Kirkmichael
744 ▲ MOUNT BLAIR
B8019
LOCH TUMMEL
Pitlochry
Ballintuim
A93
BALDUFF HILL 425 ▲
780 ▲ FARRAGON HILL
Grandtully
A827
Ballinluig
CRAIG NAM MIAL ▲ 561
A924
Bridge of Cally
Alyth
eville
Aberfeldy
B898
509 ▲ DEUCHARY HILL
Blairgowrie
Rattray
PERTH AND
A826
Dunkeld
A923
A947
A923
Coupar Ang
Quaich
A822
A984
Caputh
Burrelton
A93
A94
A92
805 ▲ MEALL NAM FUARAN
Amulree
Bankfoot
B867
Tay
KINROSS
Stanley
B9099
Guildtown
Harrietfield
B8063
Almond
LOCH TURRET
Methven
Almond
Balbeggie
B953
Gilmerton
A85
Scone
Perth
Glencarse
rie
Crieff
B9112
11
393 ▲ TORLUM
A85
10
Muthill
A823
Earn
B8062
Bridge of Earn
9
Earn
A913
Nev
B936
Auchterarder
A822 A823
Dunning
B8062
Abernethy
A822
Glenfarg
A912
M90
Auchtermuch
raco
INNERDOWNY HILL 497 ▲
DOCHRIE HILL 356 ▲
8
Falkland
A9
Greenloaning
Ochil Hills
Devon
A823
Carnbo
Kinross
7
Kinross
Kinnesswood
Glen
BEN CLEUCH 720 ▲
S
6
LOCH LEVEN
A911
blane
CLACKMANNAN-SHIRE
Powmill
B9097
Ballingry
B92
Bridge of Allan
Alva
Dollar
Cleish
5
Lochgelly
Cardend
Tillicoultry
Hill End
A823
Saline
4
Abedour
B9157
B923
Alloa
Clackmannan
Kingseat
Cowdenbeath
A909
Bu
Bannockburn
A905
Dunfermline
3
Stirling
A907
Crossford
Abedour
Dalgety Bay
S
A9
Airth
3
Kincardine
2
Inverkeithing
2
Larbert
Grangemouth
6
Bo'ness
South Queensfe
Falkirk
5
A904
M9
4

Information

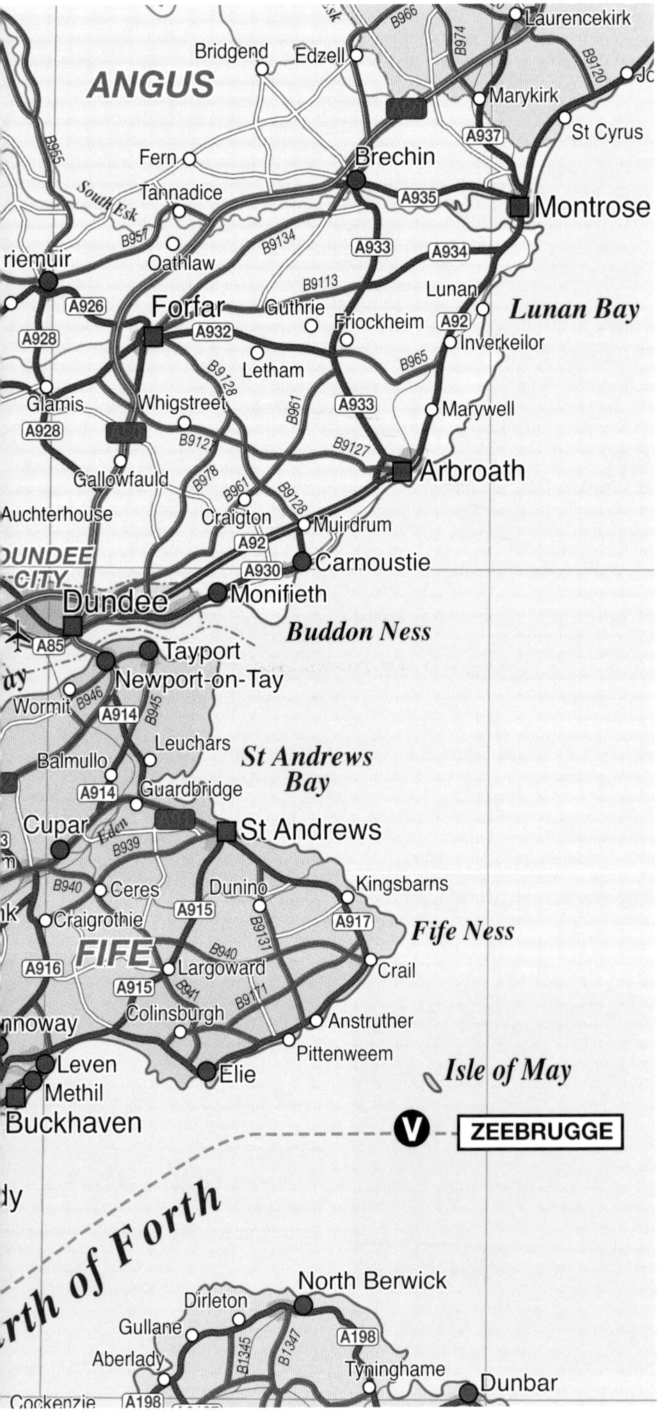

Laurencekirk
B966
B974
B9120
Bridgend
Edzell
ANGUS
Marykirk
A937
St Cyrus
B955
Fern
Brechin
South Esk
Tannadice
A935
Montrose
B957
Oathlaw
B9134
A933
A934
riemuir
B9113
Lunan
A926
Forfar
Guthrie
Lunan Bay
A928
A932
Friockheim
A92
Inverkeilor
B9128
Letham
B965
Glamis
Whigstreet
B961
A933
Marywell
A928
B9127
B9127
Arbroath
Gallowfauld
B978
B961
B9128
Auchterhouse
Craigton
Muirdrum
A92
DUNDEE
CITY
A930
Carnoustie
Dundee
Monifieth
A85
Buddon Ness
Tayport
Newport-on-Tay
Wormit
B946
A914
B945
Leuchars
St Andrews
Bay
Balmullo
A914
Guardbridge
Cupar
Eden
St Andrews
B939
B940
Ceres
Dunino
Kingsbarns
Craigrothie
A915
B9131
A917
Fife Ness
FIFE
B940
A916
Largoward
Crail
A915
B941
B9171
Colinsburgh
Anstruther
Pittenweem
Leven
Elie
Isle of May
Methil
Buckhaven
ZEEBRUGGE
rth of Forth
North Berwick
Dirleton
Gullane
A198
Aberlady
B1345
B1347
Tyninghame
Dunbar
Cockenzie
A198

Events Calendar

February
■ Kill Your Timid Notion
Festival of experimental sound and moving image held at Dundee Contemporary Arts
dca.org.uk

March
■ Dundee Women's Festival
Venues throughout the city
d-v-a.org.uk

May
■ Dundee Degree Show
Duncan of Jordanstone College of Art and Design
exhibitions.dundee.ac.uk

■ Tayside Biodiversity Festival
Venues throughout Tayside
01382 433042
taysidebiodiversity.co.uk

■ Craft Festival Scotland
Venues throughout the city
01382 388630
dundee.ac.uk/djcad/craftfest

June
■ Dundee Literary Festival
Based at Dalhousie Building, University of Dundee
01382 384413
literarydundee.co.uk

■ Angus Glens Walking Festival
Venues throughout Angus
angusahead.com/walkingfestival

■ Douglas Summer Festival
Balunie Avenue
01382 436944
dundeecity.gov.uk/events/event.php?id=3218

■ Dundee WestFest
Various venues in the West End
01382 566068
dundeewestfest.com

July
■ Dundee Blues Bonanza
Over 30 venues around the city
dundeebluesbonanza.co.uk

■ T in the Park
Balado, Kinross
tinthepark.com

■ Scottish Transport Extravaganza
Glamis Castle
svvc.co.uk

September
■ Dundee Flower and Food Festival
Camperdown Park
01382 433815
dundeeflowerandfoodfestival.com

■ Doors Open Days
Various venues throughout the city
doorsopendays.org.uk

↘ Jazz star Courtney Pine

⬃ **Food for thought** Nick Nairn dishes up at the Flower and Food Festival

■ **Angus and Dundee Roots Festival**
Various venues throughout the city
tayroots.com

■ **Airshow RAF Leuchars**
01334 839000
airshow.co.uk

October
■ **Dundee Science Festival**
Various venues throughout the city
techfestsetpoint.org.uk/activities/dundee

■ **Discovery Film Festival**
Dundee Contemporary Arts
discoveryfilmfestival.org.uk

November
■ **Dundee Jazz Festival**
Various venues throughout the city

01382 434940 (ticket sales)
jazzdundee.co.uk

■ **Dundee Mountain Film Festival**
Bonar Hall, 01828 686764
dundeemountain
film.org.uk

■ **NeON Digital Arts Festival**
Various venues throughout the city
northeastofnorth.com

December
■ **Christmas Light Night**
City Centre
dundee.com

■ **RSNO Christmas Concert**
Caird Hall
rsno.org.uk

FOR LATEST EVENTS SEE DUNDEE.COM

Information

Index

Index

Index